contents

author of this note Kate Domaille is a freelance writer
and lecturer of Media Studies. She taught in secondary schools in
London for ten years before becoming a film and video examiner at the
British Board of Film Classification. She recently completed an MA in
Media Studies where her dissertation examined developments in audience research which have enabled new questions to be raised about the
way the media is read and understood. She has contributed articles
about teaching media at A level to a number of publications.

background

trailer

In March 1998 *The Full Monty* received four academy award nominations for Best Director, Best Original Screenplay, Best Original Score and Best Picture. James Cameron's epic *Titanic* swept up most of the awards, but *The Full Monty* came away with one Oscar for best Original Score in a musical or comedy. The profile the film received through the various nominations complemented the extraordinary box office success of this low-budget British film.

At the British Academy Film and Television Awards (BAFTA) *The Full Monty* defeated *Titanic, L.A. Confidential* and *Romeo and Juliet* to the award of

Best Film and collected awards for Robert Carlyle as best actor and Tom Wilkinson as best actor in a supporting role. The film received one further award from the audience for Most Popular Film.

Since going on general release in August 1997 *The Full Monty* has won a *Screen Actor's Guild Award* for Best Cast and, at the *Evening Standard Awards*, was declared the Best Film of the Year; Robert Carlyle again picking up the best actor award.

The award ceremonies endorsed the film's phenomenal success. In February 1998, six months after the film was released, it was reported to have taken £47.8 million at the British box office, toppling the previous record of £47.7 million held by *Jurassic Park*.

From the moment *The Full Monty* was released the film achieved a unique response. Newspaper headlines greeted its first screening with a great deal of warmth and humour. Across broadsheets and tabloids the essential stripping joke was milked for humour in review headlines:

'Thong and dance', in keeping with the tone that most of the other papers took on their reviews, was the headline in *The Sunday Times* (31.8.97).

'Widgers United' read Jonathan Romney's review in *The Guardian* (29.8.97).

'Asset stripper' enjoined *The Independent* (28.8.97).

'The Bare-faced cheek of it' *The Times* (31.8.97).

'Clever Dicks' was David Gritten's headline for a later *Telegraph* article on why *The Full Monty* took everybody by surprise.

reading the full monty

Both in the title of the film and in the marketing, much was made of the men daring to go 'the full monty'. The film teases the viewer throughout that the men are going to strip and reveal all. Peter Cattaneo, the director, has been reported as saying that the element of surprise in the audience response at the end of the film was real. Over 300 extras were hired for the final scene in the nightclub. They were teased into thinking they would see the 'full monty' and then their surprise was captured in the final shot, when the cast *did* remove their hats and bare all. They are the only audience who gets to see the promise of the film's title. The external audience has to be content to share in their surprise and excitement. The joy and thrill of the final shot is that the audience is left imagining what it would have been like to have been there.

In the intial script there was no scene with the men taking their clothes off - Simon Beaufoy, the scriptwriter, just wanted to present the idea. But the producer, director and distributor were all eager to include such a scene, not just for the humour but to demonstrate the commitment of the men to bringing the project to conclusion. For although this film is primarily a comedy it is a comedy that is combined with a more serious exploration of the effects of unemployment on men in the North when traditional labour has ceased to exist. On a more serious note this film is about the ways in which a group of men attempt to recover their self-esteem by literally removing the layers of prior masculinity that have secured and protected them.

The Full Monty (directed by Peter Cattaneo and produced by Uberto Pasolini, 1997) was a runaway success film, shocking all the critics and astounding and pleasing its American distributors Fox Searchlight when it recovered its production costs in the first week of opening at the box office. The film was widely popular in Britain but even more surprising was a success in the United States, despite a strong use of English vernacular - North Country dialect.

The critical response (see Critical Responses) to the film shows that *The Full Monty* was received as a perfect realisation of British comedy and British social realism. The film was marketed as a film about male sexuality which is a rare subject in film. Billboard advertisements of a naked actor covering his private parts in one way or another were distributed nationwide to stimulate interest. The whole element of sexual tease ran right the way through the marketing campaign (see Marketing Success) and was used to good effect when the video was released in March 1998. On the cover of the video were the cast. The lettering of *The Full Monty* was made to represent the subject matter of the film with a zip at half-mast on the

quality of acting and the chemistry between the cast

giant 'M' suggesting that the film would work its way towards its notorious title: a revelation of men doing 'the full monty'.

What makes *The Full Monty* so funny is the fact that the men dare to strip for an audience, dare to go through with their scheme. It relies on a sharply written script finely performed by a strong cast led by Robert Carlyle. He acts as the instigator, persuading a group of unlikely men of different ages and shapes to join together in forming a Sheffield version of The Chippendales. The film shows how they bring together their varying needs and capabilities into a hilarious version of The Chippendales. Along the way we discover the difficulties of each of the men, how they deal with their unemployment and how they manage their feelings of social and sexual inadequacy.

key players' biographies

It is quite possible that the unified vision of the director, producer and scriptwriter was the essential formula for the success of *The Full Monty*. The high quality of acting and the chemistry between the cast has also received a great deal of positive critical attention. In 1995 Uberto Pasolini, Peter Cattaneo and Simon Beaufoy had never met or worked together but each had some knowledge and admiration of the other's work.

UBERTO PASOLINI – THE PRODUCER

In *The Sunday Times* (31.8.97) Rupert Widdicombe argued that it was Uberto Pasolini who was the 'midwife' of the film. Pasolini was a banker when he gave up his job to work as an assistant on *The Killing* Fields in 1984. Pasolini developed a working knowledge of films during the 1980s, sufficient to establish his own production company Redwave Films in 1991. He is credited with possessing the original idea for *The Full Monty* and it was he who sought the right kind of scriptwriter to develop the project.

SIMON BEAUFOY – THE SCRIPTWRITER

Beaufoy graduated from the Bournemouth Film School and had written a number of short films, an award-winning radio play and two other feature scripts before *The Full Monty*. Pasolini had seen Simon Beaufoy's script for

Among Giants, a film starring Pete Postlethwaite, and had been impressed. Beaufoy said that he wanted *The Full Monty* to be life-affirming and Pasolini made it clear that he, too, wanted the film to be more than a rendition of 1980s films criticising Margaret Thatcher. In the Introduction to the script Beaufoy says that when Pasolini suggested a film about unemployed men becoming male strippers, all kinds of strands clicked into place. He had observed the changes in male and female roles and was interested in the ways in which a lot of puzzled blokes had been left behind by the changes to sexual politics in the 1980s and 1990s, and that was to be the focus of the script: 'a tribute to all those men who are trying, manfully, to catch up'.

Pasolini's contacts at *Channel Four* put up the original funding for the script development which subsequently went through four drafts before being completed. As mentioned earlier, Beaufoy initially had not had a scene where the men removed their clothes but the financiers insisted on this as a key selling point.

Beaufoy said he wrote the script for the writer's minimum, receiving only £32,000. *The Full Monty* has, however, brought him considerable publicity and in March 1998 he finally managed to sell his six-year-old script *Among Giants* to Fox Searchlight. Beaufoy's work focuses on harder issues than Hollywood is used to dealing with. He is said to have had one script rejected because it was about the death of a child, a subject that Hollywood is none too happy to take on.

More doors have opened to him since the success of *The Full Monty* but Beaufoy is uncertain whether he wants to write scripts for the people who are now offering him support.

PETER CATTANEO – THE DIRECTOR

The Full Monty was Peter Cattaneo's début as a big screen film director. Educated at film school in Leeds, Cattaneo had a low-profile graduation. He directed a number of short films and was involved in directing drama for television – his most notable contribution was on ITV's *The Bill* during the early 1990s.

Cattaneo gained his first big break when he was given the job of directing a film in BBC2's *Love Bites* series. In 1995 Cattaneo directed *Loved Up* for the BBC. This was a film about the advantages and disadvantages of drugs, portraying the excitement and the down-side of drug use and club-culture. It was a significant film in that it sought to contextualise the use of drugs and to express both the joy and the pain of young people.

Uberto Pasolini (the producer) had seen *Loved Up* at the Sundance Festival in Utah (see Production History) and liked it. He selected Cattaneo for the role of director. Fortunately Fox Searchlight, the financiers of *The Full Monty*, had also seen and liked *Loved Up* when it was screened at Sundance and endorsed the choice of Cattaneo as director.

PAUL BUCKNOR – THE CO-PRODUCER

The role played by Paul Bucknor, the co-producer, has attracted a fair deal of controversy. Bucknor has argued in the press that the original idea for *The Full Monty* was his idea (*Observer*, 7.9.97). Such a claim is in conflict with Pasolini's who has stated that his idea 'unemployed men turn to stripping to make money' grew out of an observation of a new trend in Britain for male strippers, a challenge to traditional male/female sexual roles. Paul Bucknor is reported to have said that he first wrote a script called *Satisfaction* which was about a group of Coventry men – all black – who sought to make their living through stripping. He claims his idea was a way of exploring changes in black masculinity and sexuality. Bucknor's contention is that Simon Beaufoy's script wiped out the story about black men, replacing it with a safer, filmic version of white men.

Bucknor's claim to the original idea is not the only controversy the film has attracted. A North London playwright claimed the script was a rip-off of her play *Ladies Night* also about a group of male strippers. A bold attempt at a law suit was then made – and lost – when two New Zealand playwrights went to court with Fox Searchlight over the rights to the story which they claimed was lifted from their 1987 play.

Pasolini never claimed it to be a unique idea. In fact his pitch was really only a few words, which were developed with the assistance of *Channel Four* into a script by Simon Beaufoy. The amount of controversy over the idea does raise an interesting question about the rights to ideas. Part of the controversy is clearly over how some people's work gains recognition over others. But a great deal of argument over ideas might arise simply because the essential story is well within the bounds of ordinary narrative, that is a group of people down on their luck, struggling against all odds. Such a narrative is a recurring one in Hollywood and beyond. In this respect the basic idea for the story is like a thousand other stories. Settling the conflict over whose idea it is would be difficult. The rights to the script, however, are not in contest. Whoever held the original idea, the film was shot from the script produced by Simon Beaufoy.

the cast

Robert Carlyle (see stars) is the only major name in the cast and he does play the lead role. Cattaneo had said that he wanted the characters to look like 'ordinary blokes' which is one of the reasons for having a cast who were little known in Britain and certainly had no international currency.

the cast at the Golden Globe Awards

Many of the cast had worked together before on *Priest*, a film made by Antonia Bird for the BBC in 1994. Tom Wilkinson (Gerald in *The Full Monty*) had played the role of Father Matthew Thomas; Paul Barber (Horse in *The Full Monty*) had a cameo role; Robert Carlyle co-starred alongside Linus Roache; Lesley Sharp (Dave's wife Jean in *The Full Monty*) had played a minor role. Cattaneo seems to have largely drawn on a bank of British actors who have some currency within television or low-budget British cinema. The intention to stay within the 'ordinary bloke' remit certainly paid off at the box office. Each of the actors offered credible representations of their characters on screen.

The film made a lot of money, yet the actors all agreed at the formation of the project to work for Equity rates – yielding Steve Huison (Lomper) just £13,500 for his involvement. In Hollywood, stars command enormous fees for their participation in a project which are then met when a studio is sure the film is likely to exceed its costs at the box office. Nobody envisaged this happening with *The Full Monty*. The profits that the film accrued may not have made their way back into the pockets of the actors, but at least the publicity that the film attracted has had a beneficial effect on the work since offered to the cast, director, scriptwriter and producer.

The Full Monty was nominated for four Academy Awards (Best Director, Best Original Screenplay, Best Picture and Best Original Score). Despite its low-budget origins, and intentions to meet with a small British audience, the success it gained from the massive publicity offered by Fox Searchlight has meant that the creators of the film have achieved sufficient recognition and reward to ensure their continued success – not as a team necessarily but as successful independent players in a range of future projects.

auteur theory

When discussing literature it is usual to focus on the work of the author as the primary artistic influence on the text. The majority of works of fiction, for example, come from the ideas of a single individual and accordingly that work becomes attributed to them and their artistry is the focus of analysis. With respect to films, however, the concept of author becomes much more controversial. At the advent of cinema, nobody really credited the new art form as worthy of being attributed to one individual. Films were constructed from the efforts of many different people with varying skills. When films gained critical acclaim it was more the quality of acting and the effect of the story – that is the focus on the actual text – than it was from the way in which the text was put together. Initially film was not considered to be a worthy art form. However, acting was, having already been a well-established art form in the theatre.

In the 1950s a group of French film-makers argued that it was possible to attribute the 'look' of a film to the director and that directors were entitled to be named 'auteurs' or authors of the film. The debates between French cinema and Hollywood were about the worth of the medium, and about the right for independent expression and recognition of work created outside of the powerful Hollywood studio system which dominated film worldwide.

With respect to Hollywood production during the 'Golden Age' the concept of the 'auteur' was highly controversial. Within the strict confines of production, distribution and exchange it was not considered possible for there to be much room for individual expression and some critics argued that this was secondary to the formula success of films made within particular genres and using stars of high value.

Some film-makers and critics, however, found the concept of the 'auteur' essential as a means of marking out the quality or value of an individual director's contribution to the art. Alfred Hitchcock, for example, has acquired this treatment. While at one level Hitchcock worked within the production constraints of the studio system, it was argued that he also developed a highly recognisable style of his own. And in more contemporary times the work of Stephen Spielberg or Quentin Tarantino might attract the same kind of arguments. However, while 'auteur' theory had a certain currency in the 1950s and 1960s and assisted in giving the study of film an 'academic frame', it has not been universally embraced.

For one, *auteurism* attributes the look of a film to the director and in so doing credits that one individual with authority over the look and feel of the film. *Auteur criticism* affords academic criticism of film by describing

auteur theory background

what is characteristic about a director's work as well as assessing the quality of it. *Auteur criticism* is a significant challenge to the concept that films are produced according to formulas and governed by industrial rather than aesthetic considerations.

Even within popular genres it is possible to assess the way an individual director has made a contribution to the genre, and possibly even altered the expectations for that genre. Hitchcock developed a highly sophisticated and recognisable film style. His works, like the work of many other successful directors, became studied as examples of development in film narrative and film style.

There are a few examples of film-makers who are responsible entirely for a particular film text. Spike Lee's first feature *She's Gotta Have It* is a case in point. But the development of a director's work and the continuation of film-making is contingent on many other factors. The majority of films are a collaborative effort between producers, directors, screenwriters, actors and a largely invisible technical back-up staff. No successful film-making practice is entirely an artistic endeavour divorced from economic considerations.

Consequently in the making of a film there is a need to account for the quality of scriptwriting and the extent of the star vehicle. There is a need to have a producer capable of raising funds and ensuring the film is distributed and exhibited. The director has a clear role in bringing the film into being at an artistic level but the roles of other players are vital in bringing the film to an audience.

The Full Monty is stylistically efficient but unremarkable. In this respect it is hard to discuss Cattaneo as having a vital *auteuristic* role to play. In fact in the Foreword to the script Cattaneo pays respect to Simon Beaufoy, the scriptwriter:

> *Whilst being a very simple tale, the journey Simon takes us on is full of unexpected turns and delightful characterisation. The characters are real, distinctive and drawn with great warmth and affection ... Writing like this gives the cast everything they need to work with, – irony, character, tenderness, – and leaves a director (certainly this one) with the easiest job.*

Cattaneo shrugs off the *auteur* description. In an interview with Nick Hasted of *The Independent* (28.8.97) he argued that 'The movie is Simon Beaufoy's script ... 95 per cent of what I shot is what he wrote'.

Cattaneo also mentions Uberto Pasolini's role as being 'insightful ... a huge creative influence, to the very last cut of the film'. About his own direction, he said he cut out any jokes he didn't think were real, '... and I trod on performances, I kept them small. I wanted everything to be as real as I could make it. But everything else came from other people. I hate the idea that it is all my work, because people in America now seem to think that they can give me some second-rate script and I'll sprinkle some *Monty* dust on it. That's not the case'.

In this homage to his collaborators Cattaneo refuses the auteur title for himself. Instead he claims he had the easiest job. In Narrative and Form there is discussion of the ways in which the film owes its style to the well-established conventions of the British New Wave. However, as is argued in Contexts, the film is very much of its particular time, and Cattaneo said 'We wanted to make a working-class film that working-class people might actually go to see ... the thing we added was hope'. He defended the film's lack of closure by saying 'I think a magic had come in by that stage of the scene ... I think a freeze-frame of six-guy's genitals would have taken it from the magical to the medical, very quickly. I really wanted it to be "Wow, they did it!", not "How big are their dicks?" '

conclusion

The Full Monty has attracted a great deal of positive criticism and the film's success was clearly rewarded financially. In May 1998 it was reported that the film had grossed more than £140 million worldwide. This profit was felt by the initial investors Fox Searchlight rather than by the producers and actors. But the success of the film, which was undoubtedly due in part to Searchlight's faith in the project and expertise in distribution, has been felt across the British film industry.

British films have a poor history of global success, particularly when those films have explored issues that are essentially British. What makes *The Full Monty* almost unique in British film history is the fact that a story based

conclusion background

on unemployed steel workers, delivered by a cast of virtually unknown actors in northern vernacular, could have such a wide appeal in both making the audience laugh and at the same time think about male sexuality and masculinity in the 1990s. Its success will increase confidence in British productions and lead to a broadening out of potential investment from America.

This book offers opportunities for studying the film as a success of a clear marketing strategy and as an example of British film-making at its best. Two chapters focus on narrative and style while the last chapter deals with questions of representation, genre, intertextuality, audience theory, and the unusual production context of *The Full Monty*.

narrative & form

Cinema or film is often described as a 'closed narrative'. This means that the essential story or plot takes place over a limited amount of time, the norm is ninety minutes. Cinema, as a medium, is distinctly different from its preceding form, the novel. A novel has to both narrate and describe, and the means for achieving this is language. In film the image can both narrate and describe at the same time. Indeed the success of a film depends upon the film-maker's ability to achieve this goal. The exposition of a story cannot depend entirely on characters describing every motive or thought, though characters and how we learn about them is vital to the telling of the story. The elaboration of a plot comes from other formal and stylistic techniques. There is a specific film 'language' that has been developed and learned by the audience to enable a story to be told.

The term narrative refers to *how* stories are told and narrative theory relates to how various elements of a film, some formal and some stylistic, are brought together to create a coherent text. This chapter will outline some of the main principles and theories associated with the formal elements of film narration and how they can be applied to *The Full Monty*, while the next chapter deals more explicitly with film style.

approaches to narrative

The most influential theories of narrative focus on how narratives are structured. Tzvetan Todorov, writing in the 1960s, argued that all narratives followed a simple structure: at the beginning there is a kind of 'equilibrium' or balance. This balance becomes disrupted by an event which sets in motion a chain of other events – 'disequilibrium'. The narrative moves towards bringing these elements back into balance again: 'equilibrium'.

While this sounds quite simple, at one level – every story has a beginning, a middle and an end – Todorov's theory is intended to enable the spectator to ask questions about *how* the story is ordered. Any given story can be told in any number of ways, according to a variety of perspectives. The perspective given in a story is dependent upon how the initial equilibrium is set up – and consequently how it is disrupted and then re-ordered.

Todorov focused on the structure of events. Other theorists have argued that narratives can be ordered according to shared characteristics. Vladmir Propp's 1975 work on *The Morphology of the Folktale* (see Bibliography, Branston and Stafford's *The Media Students' Book* for a fuller account) argued that all narratives use a series of character roles and functions to drive a narrative forward. Briefly, Propp reduced all characters to eight types: hero, villain, donor, helper, princess, father figure, dispatcher and false hero.

Propp's approach helps the analyst to see that characters in narratives are not so much related to real-life characters as they are to having a function in telling a story. The recognisability of these types helps audiences to order meaning in stories. The function of characters and the relationships prescribed by those functions, that is the tension between hero and villain for example, help to shape narrative.

Claude Lévi-Strauss set out his theory of narrative on a series of thematic oppositions. The meaning of any narrative, Lévi-Strauss argued, was dependent on a conflict or tension between opposing forces. The principal idea here is that these oppositions are not just a structural or organisational tool, the oppositions are interwoven with a whole range of wider themes and ideas within a film. Applying Levi-Strauss's ideas to a film would enable the viewer to uncover some of the cultural values that have shaped the particular narrative.

Film-making is a cultural practice and the viewing of film an entertaining activity, yet film also attempts to show us a version of the world we live in. The 'manufacture' of 'the way things are' – for example, the almost ubiquitous representation of women as 'not man' – has been charged from

clearly marked as historical

time to time with being complicit with other ideological structures in society.

Film is a powerful medium and the imperative within the cinema industry has been to create an economic system of telling stories, a code that the audience can learn and understand. In the drive towards this approach, Levi-Strauss would argue that the complexity of social life is reduced to clear oppositions. Levi-Strauss then argued that what narratives do is aim to tell stories according to particular value systems. (See Bibliography, Branston and Stafford, for a fuller account.)

applying narrative theory

According to Todorov, all narratives begin with an equilibrium. The opening of *The Full Monty* is a piece of promotional film for Sheffield, shot some twenty-five years before the actual period of the rest of the film. It is clearly marked as a historical piece of film by the fact that it is not as big as the actual screen on which the rest of the film is shot and by its particular style, voice-over and the obvious period costumes and look of the city.

This particular sequence of film sets out to show a city prospering on steel, enabling young people to have money to enjoy the good life. It is a kind of false equilibrium because it is referring to another period of time. What it does serve to do, however, is suggest that the steel industry had once provided the men of Sheffield with a means of work. The viewer is then quickly dropped into disequilibrium in the second shot of the film when Gaz, Dave and Nathan are seen hunting around a derelict factory in search of rusty girders to sell. The very next scene sees Dave and Gaz stuck on a dumped car in the middle of the canal arguing about how they are to get out of the mess they are in.

By now, the central narrative question is established. How will these men get out of the mess they are in? This sets off a chain of other events – a belief that stripping might yield them some money and a recovery of dignity, the setting up of their group Hot Metal and the move through rehearsals towards a resolution which is: that the men do the strip, make the money and walk away. Todorov's theory of structure helps us to think through the chain of events in the narrative.

Propp's theories about character role and function are somewhat harder to apply here. The narrative of *The Full Monty* has a very simple structure in that there is only one single mission underlying the various motives of the key players: to strip and make money. Arguably all the male protagonists are heroes although Gaz and Dave's early actions with respect to Gerald could also be defined as villainous.

In Propp's terms hero does not mean somebody who achieves the best or the most commendable thing, rather it means a character who has an active role in taking the events of the story forward. Gaz is the main protagonist so arguably occupies this role most fully, but Dave and Gerald also have a need to restore self-esteem.

The role of Nathan, Gaz's son, is significantly different in that he represents a form of help to his father in achieving his goal: he acts as 'donor', someone who traditionally gives an object with magical property, but here might be translated as the one who provides money to book the club, and the 'magical' property of trust and faith in his father's endeavours. Nathan also could be described as a 'helper' in Propp's terms or even a 'dispatcher', his actions motivating Gaz's continuation with the scheme despite all the setbacks. One character can occupy more than one role.

In Levi-Strauss's terms the narrative is organised along key oppositions: employment versus unemployment; men versus women; those inside society and those outside of it; Chippendale men and northern Men. The problem for Gaz and Dave and the rest of the protagonists is that they develop a fascination for something they are not. The conflict this creates helps to structure the narrative: how will the northern men become like Chippendales?; how will unemployment be turned into employment? and how will men adopt the practices of women?

There is much to be gained from these Structuralist approaches to narrative: each theory enables the analyst to examine the role of character, the presentation of theme and the way the cause-effect system has been established.

According to the American film analyst David Bordwell (1985) these structures show that narration in the fiction film has developed according to certain conventions. The conventional narrative system was created in Hollywood, as an efficient method for telling complex stories. Bordwell argued that most Hollywood productions (even in contemporary cinema) are organised along particular lines: there is usually a plot centred around a 'star' and the plot is moved by a series of cause-and-effect relationships.

Within the classic Hollywood narrative code this involved a double-plot structure which linked a romance with another sphere of action (business, crime, adventure) and which usually brought the story to a close through romantic fulfilment. This system was highly efficient and governed the production of narratives coming out of the Hollywood studio system up until the 1950s. So efficient is the system that it continues to govern the structure of most conventional films made today.

The Full Monty does appear, in the main, to adhere to this system. The plot is centred around a main character, Gaz, played by Robert Carlyle. There is a consistent set of cause-and-effect relationships. Gaz, Dave, Gerald, Lomper, Horse and Guy all have a need to make money and the move to create a stripping troupe is predicated on that need.

There is a distinct lack of explicit romance although the state of heterosexual marriage is definitely a motif within the film. Gerald actually loses his wife within the time span of this narrative, due to his weakness at admitting the truth. Jean and Dave's marriage is fraught with difficulty. Dave's 'impotence' is the main reason for him fearing the strip but it is also the main reason for him eventually going through with it. Dave has a dual motive for agreeing to stay involved: he needs to become an 'employed' man and a successful husband again.

Gaz appears to have no wish to redeem himself with Mandy, his ex-wife, but 'impressing' her as a responsible ex-partner and father is a vital motivation for the strip. She is in the audience, at the end providing the approving 'gaze' (see Contexts, Spectatorship Theory). In this respect the film does have a kind of romantic ending albeit differently realised to the conventional Hollywood cinema closure the audience is more used to.

narrative time & space

The American cinema critic David Bordwell described media narratives as a chain of events in a cause-effect relationship occurring in time and space. Though *The Full Monty* was very favourably reviewed, one recurring criticism was that the film's chronology and temporal order limited the way the broad themes of the film – unemployment, masculinity – were brought to an exuberant but unsatisfactory resolution. There was little sense of what was to happen to these men after the strip. Would they return to the disequilibrium we first found them in? How large a resolution was this for the state of 1990s masculinity?

It has already been stated that the cause-effect relationship is quickly established in the opening scenes of the film. The men are broke and they are looking for a scheme to counteract that. The scheme Gaz comes up with is a small-time scheme and the time-scale in the film reflects this. The entire film covers a time-span of only a few weeks.

In a film the time and events are usually special to the particular story and do not have to resemble a time span in the viewer's world. Films frequently manipulate time if the story requires the narrative to cover a large time span. In a biopic, for example, the narrative may need to make use of both flashback and flashforward to elaborate missing features in the film. *The Full Monty* moves forward in time in a straight line. One event follows the other to a conclusion. In terms of time this means that a few weeks activity is compressed into ninety minutes of film-making and what the narrative does is show this in episodes. In the following example it is possible to see that each new scene establishes a question for the next and this structure drives the narrative forward:

Scene One:	What Sheffield used to be like (promotional film).
Scene Two:	What the Steel Industry is like now – defunct.
Scene Three:	What this situation has made men like.
Scene Four:	How this situation is in contrast with 'new masculinity': The Chippendales.

| Scene Five: | Considering new masculinity as a money-making scheme and so on. |

Towards the end of the film, specific time is mentioned: 'only two weeks to rehearse', 'dress rehearsals tomorrow', 'today is Monday, performance is Friday'. The mention of time and how it is related to the next event helps to order the narrative.

Likewise narrative space has a special significance. Narrative space and how it is manipulated is a vital audio-visual code that helps to create ambiguities or to clarify enigmas and to direct emotional responses to the story in particular ways. Recognising the narrative space helps the viewer to understand the ways in which the story or the characters relate to the space. Narrative space has both a real and emotional function. The question of narrative space is also linked to mise-en-scène (the setting/scenery) which is dealt with in more detail in the next chapter.

characters

In the opening stages of the film the unity of Gaz and Dave is demonstrated ironically by their exclusion from a working space. The attempt to bring together a viable strip troupe is, at first, conducted within the space of the factory. It is the site of the first rehearsals and it remains the site of subsequent ones. In this derelict space the men reconstruct themselves as workers. They adopt some of the significance of the space, a place of work, to validate their mission. Likewise the use of Gerald's house functions to assist the idea that he is involved in this stripping troupe in an attempt to hang on to some of his respectability. The nightclub is a place of work for 'performers'.

The supermarket as a space is also worthy of mention. It is a repeated space in the film and represents something quite significant, a key employer of women and a marginal employer of men. For a brief period of time in the film Dave actually gains employment in the supermarket as a security guard. The fact that this is marginal to the plot reflects the fact that it is not a suitable replacement for work in manufacturing industry which was a major employer of working-class men until relatively recently. Certain

characters

significance of space

narrative spaces are repeated in the film and this enables the viewer to quickly attribute significance to the space. But variation of that significance is also a vital aspect of moving a narrative forward.

The factory is a place of dereliction but it has another function as a place of resurrection of self-esteem and worth. It is necessary to view the significance of space with respect to characters and how they act within that space. This approach gives us information about their emotional state.

We first see Lomper, very briefly, right at the beginning of the film when he returns from his brass band performance to lock Gaz and Dave into the factory. It is this enforcement, this reminder of being locked into work that arguably sets the events in motion. We meet Lomper properly later, when he is attempting to kill himself in a car. This desperate scene, locked into a car, in a tight space, reflects Lomper's emotional torment. The next scene, shows the men outside and therefore 'alive' but tightly framed into close-ups. Men have been traditionally filmed in respect to external signifiers like cities and work places to illustrate their position in the world. The 'outside' location is not exploited in this film and reflects the men's exclusion from the workplace and from the world.

Gerald is seen in a wider range of locations, partly to signify his previously stronger position in the world. Gerald first appears in the job club, sitting apart from the more disenfranchised group of men. He is making a more determined effort to restore his working life, at first. He is next seen in the community hall, dancing with his wife to keep up appearances that he still has a position in the world. We next see him in a job interview where Gaz and Dave are clearly outside of such possibilities. Eventually Gerald concedes his exclusion by joining Gaz and Dave on the panel in the factory. It is an admission of his need to resurrect his working status through Gaz and Dave's initiative.

Both Horse and Guy appear for the first time in the factory rehearsals intent on using the space to revive their fortunes. They are led through the initiative by Gaz, Dave and Gerald who have the motive of earning money to the fore at all times. Horse and Guy represent more of the same type of men – unemployed men – desperate for a quick solution to their crisis (see Contexts, Genre, for more on this). This sequence of introductions accords to a common means of representing the various characters: a central role, cameo role and supporting roles – Gaz as the central figure, Dave and Gerald as cameo roles and Lomper, Horse and Guy as supporting roles.

The characters share a common purpose, that of returning to work. However, they also have diverse needs –keeping contact with his son (Gaz) or holding on to his marriage (Dave). We are shown their various needs through the diversity of representation. We have old and young, slim and fat, gay and straight, black and white characters.

The characters each occupy a different position on the spectrum of masculine need. The story is deliberately playing with spectator interpretations of character roles and actions. This film is not just about male unemployment, it is about the different ways that position is conceived and felt by men.

Initially, given his overt chauvinism and obvious fecklessness, it is difficult to accept Gaz as a hero. Yet he is developed as a character of considerable moral integrity, signified primarily by his relationship with his son, Nathan, and his quest to hold on to that. Dave fluctuates between complicity with Gaz and cowardice, fear of revealing his true self. This is signified by his move in and out of a security guard's costume and demonstrates his desire for respectable employment and a return to a happy and fulfilling marriage.

The costumes of all of the characters accord with what one might expect from men of their age and social standing. Costume does have a realist function but it also functions to demonstrate their various positions. Gaz's 'leather jacket', for example, accords with the way he is broadly perceived. When caught putting up posters publicising their act, Gaz is addressed by a young woman as 'Garry the lad'. Gaz's clothing, gestures and overt chauvinistic comments all lead us to 'read' him as a 'lad'.

Gerald's clothes are equally vital for how we are to 'read' him. In part through the clothes he wears, shirt, tie, jumper and anorak, Gerald deludes his wife that he is still in employment. Learning to remove this disguise is part of Gerald's learning to face the truth about his situation. Only when he is literally stripped bare and the police arrest him, does his charade of still being in employment become uncovered. He returns from the police station to find the contents of his house being removed.

Lomper's clothes are ill-fitting, distinctly unfashionable, and reflect his social awkwardness. Conversely Guy's clothes show his sexual prowess, tight-fitting jeans, underwear that befits his status as 'the lunchbox'. The clothing of the characters is essential to how we understand them.

Essentially the understanding of character is achieved by how they are positioned with respect to narrative space as much as by what is revealed by aspects of narrative style (covered in the next chapter) and by dialogue.

restricted/omniscient narration

Another aspect of how narratives are constructed is the voice-telling of the story. The majority of films are told in 'third-person' narration where the film seems to be told in an impersonal way, as if someone just happened to be there to observe a story unfolding. This omniscient narration is true of *The Full Monty*.

Having said that the emphasis on the troupe is very uneven. The spectator is invited into the personal crises of Gaz, Dave and Gerald, while the more specific problems of Lomper, Horse and Guy gain only minor elaboration.

Arguably the story is very much told from the point of view of Gaz. He occupies most scenes and he is the driving force behind the idea to form the strip. His motive is given precedence above all others because his son, Nathan, also occupies an important role in the film.

The question of point of view with respect to style is dealt with more fully in the next chapter, Style, but it is worth describing here just how much of the story belongs to Gaz. From the outset Gaz's access to his son is threatened. The maintenance arrears are mentioned a number of times and the threat to his being able to see Nathan gathers pace as the story progresses. It is Gaz who begs Dave to get involved, who co-opts Lomper into the troupe, who chases Gerald all over town and establishes the auditions. It is Gaz who arranges costumes, books the nightclub, organises the publicity and brings it to its natural conclusion.

The camera dwells significantly on Gaz's regular struggles with his ex-wife and his son. His point of view is both comically and poignantly illustrated when he stands in a separate dole queue to the rest of the troupe and watches their rehearsals with amusement and pride. We see the other men through Gaz's eyes (see Contexts, Spectatorship Theory).

While the dominant point of view belongs to Gaz, the narrative also follows Dave's fears about the loss of his masculinity socially and sexually, and Gerald's quest to hang on to his middle-class aspirations.

Though it does use a traditional third-person narrative approach, the style (see Style) helps to privilege the perspectives and viewpoints of these characters over any wider viewpoint. The structure of the characterisation works in conjunction with the use of narrative space and certain stylistic features and helps to shape the story.

sound

A much underestimated aspect of narrative is the use of sound. Dialogue clearly contributes significantly to the shape and style of the narrative. Characters carry the story forward through what they say and how they bring about the particular journey through the disequilibrium. But this particular film also makes significant use of a soundtrack which has both a formal and stylistic function. The stylistic effects of the soundtrack are given more space in the following chapter. In terms of the narrative, however, the music in this film is used to cut across episodes and assist the audience in making connections between one part of the story and another.

The Full Monty does have an original film score which runs almost continuously. It makes use of a range of traditional 'brass band' instrumentation and is therefore fitting for the themes of the film. However, the film also makes extensive use of a soundtrack, from Errol Brown's 'You Sexy Thing' and a range of other 1970s' hits to Tom Jones's powerful rendition of 'You Can Keep Your Hat On'. For the most part the music assists the comprehension

film appropriates music from the past. The music is borrowed from a period of better prosperity and from a time when the roles of men and women were more distinct. This use of music has a significant function in terms of assisting the various moves across the narrative from chauvinistic men to 'new man'.

The Chippendales dance to Donna Summer's 'Hot Stuff' and to Gary Glitter's 'Do You Wanna Be In My Gang?'. The lyrics that are heard from these songs accord with the actions the songs accompany. 'Hot Stuff' becomes an aspirational song within the film – these men have to become 'Hot Stuff'. The song is heard in their rehearsals and is most memorably used when they coordinate their routine in the dole queue. Other music helps to shape the ways in which we see the men shift their values. Gerald, for example, moves away from the respectability of the tango towards Flashdance which he argues is 'just a souped up tango'.

The intertextual (see Contexts, Intertextuality) value of Flashdance varies according to the age of the audience but if recognised it functions for a number of reasons: the actress Jenifer Gray takes the role of a welder and dancer and symbolises precisely what the men have been and will be. The song 'What a Feeling', begins 'At first there is nothing ... but a slow glowing dream' and as this is heard right at the beginning of the plan, it fits well with the place the men are at.

Later in the film other music assists the comprehension of what is going on. 'You've done it all, you've broken every code', the opening lines of Cockney Rebel's hit 'Come Up And See Me' accords with the new bonding of the men in their common purpose and is played in the scene where the men are trying keep-fit exercises outside. At Gerald's house, in the scene in Linda's bedroom the unity of the men is reinforced with the Sister Sledge track 'We are Family'.

If music is used to reinforce the action, it also has a vital function in demonstrating the awkwardness of their plan. The use of 'Je t'Aime' by Jane Birkin and Serge Gainsbourough is in direct contrast to Reg's feelings about stripping when they first establish the auditions. Gaz notably cuts the soundtrack short to prevent Reg suffering any futher humiliation. Likewise the theme tune for stripping is tuneless and jarring when they cannot

opening/closes

coordinate their movements. It is played properly by a brass band later to show support for Lomper's part in the venture.

If there is any doubt as to the efficiency of the music then it can be tested against the final use of music. Tom Jones is a significant choice of performer. He represents a particular brand of masculinity, grown from his ability to impress a female audience through his singing and his particular expression of male virility and strength. His song 'You Can Keep Your Hat On' appropriately awards the men the respect they deserve for while they do not literally keep their hats on, the final message of the film is that they have earned respect again.

opening/closes

To test most of the theory that has been described here it is worth spending some time thinking through what the beginning and end points of a film are, and thereby contemplating how one was taken to the resolution. At the beginning of *The Full Monty* we are presented with two characters who discover that women have changed, that they are willing and able to pay men for entertaining them via a traditional means by which women have entertained men – stripping.

When Gaz first mentions in the job club that 'Eh, Dave, it's worth a thought though', the narrative is set properly in motion. A number of enigmas or puzzles have to be resolved. How will Gaz and Dave change their thinking about male and female roles and learn the necessary dance steps to follow through their plan? How will they get together a group of willing other men? Where will they practice? What skills will they need to learn? How will they turn local women's attention away from The Chippendales version of masculinity towards admiring their own unique brand of it?

The way time is compressed in the narrative is via these kinds of episodes. The narrative is closed at the point of their doing the strip because this befits the narrow focus they have come up with for resolving their own dilemmas. The film does not attempt to deal with the more pressing long-term questions of how men adapt to unemployment. It deals with how they will resolve the crisis of the minute: for Gaz that is getting together £700 for maintenance arrears; for Dave it is impressing Jean and resuming his role as a sexual partner in their marriage; for Gerald it is about testing his fears of loss of status; for Lomper it is about making friends and forging an entry into a mature adult life, separated from his mother. For Horse and Guy the motive is never clearer than that they wish to make a quick buck. The closure of the film then accords with the minor purpose of their task and is much more in keeping with the film's primary purpose as a comedy rather than a slice of social realism.

conclusion

This chapter has outlined many developments in the theory of narrative and how stories are told in film. It has put emphasis on the importance of certain kinds of conventions of storytelling and how these conventions enable viewers to 'read' films. With respect to *The Full Monty* the arguments made here are that the film accords with a conventional narrative system – the telling of a story in a linear fashion, the progression of a story through time, and the ways in which certain aspects of space and character as well as sound have assisted in adding meaning to the dialogue. The chapter, Style, that follows is about how aspects of film style assist in communicating meaning and pleasure to the audience.

style

One of the central objectives of film analysis is to unravel the ways in which certain clearly encoded images carry meaning for the audience. A key theoretical development in the twentieth century has been the ways in which language has both a descriptive and social meaning. Within the discipline of semiotics particularly, the aim has been to demonstrate that language has a denotative (descriptive) and connotative (social) function.

While simple words like 'man' clearly describe the figure of a male human being, connotative aspects of the way that man is represented to us reveal something more specific about social standing, age, position, etc. Within film, it is the extraneous signifiers (mise-en-scène, clothing, lighting, framing, angles, sound) that enable the audience to read certain significances of location and character. Narratives are distinguished from each other by this use of style, drawing attention to actions and dialogue in keeping with what the film is trying to say.

The style of a film is contingent upon a number of factors: some of these are clearly economic – whether the film requires elaborate sets, costumes and special effects; others aesthetic – the quality of light, the design of set and costume; political – what the film is trying to say. The style of *The Full Monty* is no exception. According to Duncan Petrie (Street: 1997:117) the low economic base of British cinema has meant that there has always been more emphasis in British film on dialogue and characterisation than on mise-en-scène or montage. *The Full Monty* is in this tradition. A low budget film grown from an original screenplay in a realist tradition and in need of no special effects.

While less emphasis is on high-tech visual features, there are nevertheless vital aspects of the film's style necessary to animate the dialogue and to encourage or create support for the characters. The specific film style on which it draws, in part is that of social realism and the British New Wave.

british new wave

In 1951 the British Board of Film Censors established a specifically adult category of film – the 'X'. The response by British film-makers to this new category, was a spate of socially realist films – the horror of real life rather than the horror of horror stories. The move towards socially realist films grew from a range of influences. Firstly these films owe a debt to the documentary movement headed by John Grierson in the 1930s (Higson, 1997). The documentary movement combined the imperative to give information or instruction with innovative film-making practices. Indeed Grierson argued for a kind of 'poetic realism' combining surface details and iconography with stylistic devices that make the ordinary look strange or beautiful or poetic.

The second key influence on the New Wave was the new writing in the post-war period – novels and plays for theatre – which were essentially about the experiences of the working class, told from its perspective. The elements of style in the documentary movement were combined with new narratives about working-class identity and masculinity in cinema of the 1950s and 1960s. The Free Cinema Movement was a group of directors who had honed their talents in documentaries made in the 1950s. It was the transference of style from documentary to fiction film that is the most significant feature of these 'kitchen-sink' dramas. British cinema is not renowned for its emphasis on film as spectacle and the title 'kitchen-sink drama' supports this view in suggesting that these films focused on drab realist features rather than exploiting the visual potential of the medium. The Free Cinema Movement led by the director Lindsay Anderson wanted films to be personal statements, giving the director total control to celebrate what they called 'the poetry of the everyday'.

The style of the British New Wave was one which combined a kind of authenticity and documentary realism with a 'romantic atmosphere' or 'poetic quality', giving ordinary people narratives of worth and creating the view of the working-class as rounded people with complex social and emotional lives. Films made using this style attempted to challenge the spectacle of Hollywood. The New Wave directors sought to put the narrative before the visual. This is not to say that the films did not have their own aesthetic value, but is to say that the style was subordinate to the story and the ideas that the film was attempting to represent.

REALISM AS STYLE

The style of the New Wave then had distinctive features. The first is that films made a claim for surface realism in shooting the action on location, rather than in studios. The majority of films made in the pre-war years were always centred around the more prosperous and less industrial south of Britain. Many of the films in this period were shot in the industrial north of England. The use of these location shots was to assist the reading of the film as part of a broader narrative about the class system in Britain, to demonstrate the divide in British society. Shots of the north of England were not just a neutral narrative space, they had wider historical significance representing on screen part of a wider story about masculinity and social class. That wider significance was referenced through the locations.

The use of locations and minor stars contributed to a surface realism, likewise realistic lighting and mise-en-scène all added to the look of the film as a realist text. The derogatory term 'kitchen-sink' refers to the ways in which ordinary objects became a vital part of the mise-en-scène in New Wave films.

The rationale for using less well-known actors was that if the characters looked real then they could 'act real'. The actors, it was felt, ought to look like the characters they were playing rather than themselves. If the audience was to believe in the character then they should not become confused by their prior feelings about the star. The emphasis on authentic speech patterns was also a signficant turning away from a tradition of film-making that had been led by the need to be an international medium. Gone were the plummy English tones and in their place was the vernacular and authentic accent of the working-class man. All of these shifts constitute a clear move away from set design, studios and the 'Hollywood' nature of film-making.

A further throw back to the documentary tradition and a distancing technique from the film as spectacle was that films of the New Wave reverted to black and white photography, and grainy images. Again this constituted a deliberate shift away from the 'look' of Hollywood films. With certain aspects of style removed it was argued that the focus of the audience could remain on character and story rather than on aspects of style or effect. Black and white is a documentary convention and this technique added to the sense of authenticity, a sense of filming things as they really are.

New Wave films did borrow the narrative structure from Hollywood – broadly episodic narratives. The process of narrating a story episodically always leaves new questions unanswered. As any given scene or shot opens up new questions the narrative is driven forward. The New Wave directors argued that Hollywood's emphasis on stars and on well-accomplished style meant that the audience could be more impressed by the look of a film than by what it was attempting to say. The New Wave style aimed to reverse this process by subordinating style to narrative and drawing the viewer's attention to story rather than effect. It is a style that has arguably left the British Film Industry struggling to compete with Hollywood ever since.

While films of the Free Cinema Movement and the New Wave attracted considerable critical acclaim, it is not entirely clear whether the motivations of the film-makers were felt by the audiences of the time or since. The British New Wave films were essentially a genre about men and the ways in which working-class men felt trapped by their position in their world. Many of the films had frustrated endings where the hero might move on but where circumstances remain unchanged. At best these films offered individual solutions rather than dealing with broader social questions. There is only a partial resolution offered to the problem faced by the characters.

KEN LOACH

The film-maker Ken Loach began his career in the 1960s in television. His first film for television was a dramatised documentary called *Cathy Come Home* which drew on many aspects of the documentary movement

british new wave

style, yet sought to take the style on further to make a more detailed commentary of socio-economic and cultural life and how it impinged on individual consciousness. Loach's work over the past forty years has been consistent in its focus on representing working-class life and the ways in which opportunities for working-class people have been curtailed by socio-economic forces.

One of the most celebrated of Loach's early films is *Kes* which was made on location. But while *Kes* shares some of the stylistic qualities of the New Wave it also represents a significant challenge to New Wave films. For one, he makes a child rather than a man the focus of attention and in doing so raises key questions about childhood, about working-class educational achievement, about working-class life and about personal fulfilment within a society steeped in prejudice and pessimism. It attempts, therefore, to comment on a wider range of issues. *Kes* was shot in colour and much attention lavished on the beauty of nature and landscape as a means of representing the hope and fulfilment Billy Casper craves. Loach was keen to express working-class experience beyond working life.

Loach's work has developed and continued successfully into the 1990s and his films have explored many dimensions of British socio-economic life. He has clearly drawn on the British New Wave style, but his films place a much stronger emphasis on a gallery of characters and closer attention to the personal as well as political. Loach has commented more recently that making films in a style that explores the personal response to life is a political action:

> Fiction is about more than a political analysis, which can be very dry. Fiction is about the expression or the line on somebody's face when something happens. It's about the way light falls in a room. It's about the way people walk down the street after a lifetime's work. It's about how they live in their rooms, how they've got food on their table. It's about the fabric of life, the product of all those details of the way we are. Politics is implicit in all that, but it can't be dragged out. (See Bibliography.)

In this respect the work of Ken Loach and arguably Peter Cattaneo, the director of *The Full Monty* is a departure from the New Wave philosophy in that there is a great deal of emphasis on film style and the capacity of film style to reveal aspects of plot and character that cannot be elicited through the script alone. Loach's comments are very much about the importance of the camera, the emphasis on location, on mise-en-scène, the effect of framing, camera angles, the use of sound, editing and so on. None of these systems for producing meaning operates alone in a film, they work together, complement each other to provide a range of possible readings and interpretations.

style of the full monty

The Full Monty owes a debt to the British New Wave and the tradition of social realism, but it also offers a new way of looking at old issues. There is a great deal of focus in the film on the 'kitchen-sink' iconography. Much of the action takes place in a broken factory. But Cattaneo's film is a more celebratory rendition of what men do to cope with their immediate circumstances and some of the more 'poetic' cinematography has a lot in common with Loach's style.

Part of an audience's ability to understand films comes from the way the audience naturally measures one film experience against another (see Contexts, Intertextuality). Like other socially realist films *The Full Monty* is a film that is predominantly about working-class life, but the fact that it was made in the mid 1990s (released two months into a new Labour government) means that it reflects in part the debates of the moment.

Films in the 1980s in this vogue tended to take up the issues of restructuring work (see Contexts for more detail). This film responds to debates about the ways in which the new world order will be played out and felt. It is much more closely focused on the politics of identity than it is about the structure of work and the workplace. Consequently, its style reflects a shift in values and the following two essays, focused on film style, argue that the film is both part of the New Wave tradition and a clear departure from it.

In his introduction to the film script Simon Beaufoy argues that he wanted to write a script that was about all the men left behind in the surge towards identity politics, a film about 'the socio-political gender shifts of the late twentieth century'. Explicit in the script is the imperative for men to 'shape up, get fit, get smart and get sexy'. The question this essay addresses is how the stylistic elements of the film bring these themes out.

LOCATION

The British New Wave directors sought to make location important, with a firm emphasis on northern landscape as representative of 'authentic' working-class life. The north of England was dominated by heavy industry – coal mining, steel-making, textiles.

The Full Monty is based in Sheffield, but the external landscape in the film is less prominent than internal locations. Without the opening promotional film showing Sheffield as a once vibrant city, the film would lack a direct reference to its location. In fact the clearest establishment of location comes from shots of the renowned Meadowhall shopping centre which contributes to the new direction of industry in the North, away from engineering and manufacture and on to commerce.

Films frequently invest significance in details like place names. Sheffield used to be associated with steel-making. Steel-making was a male-dominated industry. In the films of the New Wave there was a great deal of emphasis on male physicality – how the work was done. In *The Full Monty*, however, there is a very different emphasis on physicality as the film raises a very different set of questions about how men use their bodies to make a living.

Sheffield then is stripped of its significance by placing the opening shot of the promotional film in immediate juxtaposition with an image of two men and a boy (Gaz, Dave and Nathan) hunting around a derelict factory for a rusty girder to steal and sell.

The British New Wave of Directors sought to place men in the industrial context to highlight how important the external world was for men: a place of public interactions. This film removes men predominantly from any location one normally expects to see them in. There is very little attempt to incorporate scenes of the city itself. Indeed nearly all scenes of the city are shot in long-shot and are out of focus as if what the city represented is now very far away from the realities of these men's lives.

playing with audience expectation

This stylistic device, which is also a narrative device – a refusal to place men in the external world – does much to draw attention to the internal lives of the men. What this film is more about is private grief, pain and anguish. The industrial landscape is almost entirely absent, partly to reflect the actual absence of an industrial world that employs men. The viewer is only reminded by the use of the derelict factory location that there was once a working life for these men.

Instead we see men in a whole array of other locations that are not traditionally expected of them. The film is, therefore, playing with audience expectation, with entrenched social values and beliefs. For instance, in the first half of the film we see nearly all the characters in locations that are more usually associated with children. It is no accident that Dave, Gaz and Nathan are hardly separated in the first few scenes. Their lives are intertwined, and mucking about is a daily activity for Gaz and Dave. Men's lives resemble those of children: hanging around in derelict factories, getting locked in, mucking around on a canal, walking through playgrounds and up hills, sitting at desks in a 'classroom' at the job club.

Gerald's 'managerial' status is only reinforced by his being seen at a dance class (a more adult activity) than where the other players are, sitting in a nursery annexe. In this scene Dave even gets a small plastic toy hoop stuck around his wrist. Both the location and his activity reinforce that childishness.

Men in this film are not seen in public places, not viewed in terms of work. Dave is briefly seen in Asda working as a security guard but he appears to be doing nothing at all. Even The Chippendales are not shown at work. The viewer has a sense that they are playing in the club at the beginning of the film but they are not shown 'at work'.

The majority of the film is shot indoors – inside a derelict factory, inside Gerald's house, inside a job centre club, inside a nightclub. The men are only occasionally shot in a much wider landscape: running up a hill, playing football while the city is actually out of focus behind them. This stylistic feature is important. It ensures that the viewer is aware of the effect of removing men from the workplace.

FRAMING

Linked to this question of location is the whole question of framing. The framing of a film refers to the composition of shot, what is seen in the frame and how much attachment we are expected to have with the shot. Framing has a significant effect in this film. In the scene in the toilets, for example, the women characters are all in the same frame, crowded towards a mirror. Jean's friends swap between teasing her about a man fancying her at work and then comforting her about her anguish about Dave having 'given up'.

The tight framing of the women suggests their emotional intimacy and the way they are framed is in direct contrast to the framing of the male characters at first. A similar scene of bonding is when Gaz, Dave and Lomper are lying on the grass looking up at the sky contemplating the most efficient way to kill themselves. Each is shot individually, suggesting that they are far less able to support each other emotionally than the women are.

It is worth tracking the ways in which this framing shifts as the film develops. The troupe starts as a two-some (always with Nathan in tow) and then become three, four, and eventually six in frame. It takes a long time for the men to build this unity, both in terms of what they are trying to achieve but also in terms of how they might manage to support each other's fears and anxieties. The scene in Gerald's house shows five of them stood together in underwear and socks seeing off the bailiffs from taking Gerald's television. It is a unique moment of strength and one from which all gain a great deal of support and comfort. Framing has helped the audience to read the characters' unity and disunity which is a central part of the narrative.

CAMERA ANGLES

To elaborate the second theme – one about dignity and self-esteem – the director has drawn on other important stylistic features. Ken Loach has argued it is important to draw attention to 'the lines on faces'. This film places considerable emphasis on internal anguish and consequently makes extensive use of the close-up, an important camera shot to reveal emotional depth.

camera angle style

In general, *The Full Monty* is quite simply shot. It is a low-budget comedy about ordinary life and the plot does not command a very elaborate technical code. Nevertheless it is a very deliberate choice of style to shoot the characters in close-up in the main, with the intention to elaborate each of the men's personal crises and dilemmas.

The close-up is a well-recognised piece of film code, reserved for facial expression and showing inner feelings and pain. Gaz's fear of losing contact with his son is given more prominence when the camera dwells on the pained expression he shows as his access visits come under threat. When Nathan complains that 'real dad's don't do that', Gaz squeezes closely up to the bars of the school gate and shouts 'Oo aah Cantona' through at his son who has turned away from him and then zooms in on his pained expression as he shouts 'stuff 'em Nath'.

This shot of Gaz's pain is repeated at a number of other points: in the factory rehearsals when Reg remarks that 'it's no place for kids', and again when he tries to meet Nathan from school later. The close-up gives intensity to his suffering and reminds the viewer that despite the apparent absurdity of his stripping mission, his reasons for wanting to do it are good.

The camera introduces each of the male characters one by one. They are all given the initial benefit of the close-up. Lomper's initiation into Gaz and Dave's company – after they have saved him from a suicide attempt – is heralded with a scene in which each deliberates the best possible methods of killing themselves in individual close-up. All the major introductions and revelations about character are delivered via close-up. Gerald's desperation about hiding his unemployment from his wife, his despair at the interview going wrong, his despondency as he receives the mended gnome, all the poignant moments showing his character are given in close-up.

Likewise Dave's anguish is expressed through close-up and it reaches its peak when having to confront his impotence in one of the final scenes with Jean. Jean mistakes the discovery of the leather thong as evidence that Dave is having an affair. Dave, broken by the charge, reveals in close-up 'Jean, who wants to see *this* dance?' and her reply 'Me, Dave' also delivered in close-up brings into view the extent of the sadness in their marriage at that moment.

After being rescued by Gaz and Dave, Lomper retreats into a background role. He and Guy are only briefly shot in a medium close-up to show their growing relationship. This is touched upon by the film but not as a driving force of the plot. Guy is a more minor character who is represented as more of a survivor. He, after all, possesses the only body worth looking at in conventional terms! He is almost always shot in mid-shot and we have little sense of any other motive bar money for getting involved. Like Horse he is presented without a personal history or specific motive for getting involved in the plan.

Both these characters, one gay and the other black, exist more in terms of what they may represent socially than how they are coping personally (see Contexts for more on this). Horse is only shot in close-up when he is having a tense phone call about how to use his penis enlarger.

mise-en-scène

Mise-en-scène is a French term and comes from theatre set design. Essentially it means: what is in the scene. The way a scene is shot and the way it is framed has an effect on how it is viewed. Likewise features of the shot: the use of furniture, quality of lighting, costume, etc. have a bearing on how a film is 'read'. These aspects of design also have a function in terms of elaborating certain themes and ideas. For a film about male stripping the mise-en-scène is almost entirely inappropriate for the subject but this inappropriacy has a distinctive function.

The improbability of this initial duo putting a strip group together is reinforced by the mise-en-scène. Gaz first does the calculations of how much such a scheme would earn in the job club after seeing how many women were screaming at The Chippendales in the working-men's club. In this grey room, two characters hatch the first seeds of their plan. The mise-en-scène implies such glory is a long way away from where they are sitting. Gradually Gaz sets about creating the right environment for the plan to come to fruition.

The idea grows in probability when Gaz strikes a dramatic pose in front of the headlights of a car. The mise-en-scène is far from right but this time the bright lights of the car and the playing of 'You Sexy Thing' by Hot Chocolate lend more credibility to the idea. The mock-up stage is enough to encourage Gaz's imagination and to develop his idea further.

The scheme gathers speed when they establish rehearsals to expand their group. The dimly lit and stark location of the old factory helps to support the theme, that it would indeed be difficult for this group to pull off something so elaborate. The first candidate, Reg, fails to achieve a strip in this environment. He is too desperate and too ashamed. Horse, on the other hand, appears to use the space to show what he was once capable of – nifty footwork. Guy imagines the space as a film set, but the viewer is quickly reminded that such fantasies have no place, as he falls heavily to the floor in his 'Singing In The Rain' routine. Like Horse, however, he has another asset to offer and dropping his trousers to a bunch of down-at-heel blokes in a factory does not seem to constitute a loss of dignity for Guy. It is as if, at first, this environment suggests exactly that there is no lower place to go.

Consequently the old factory becomes an important new space where new endeavours, made from broken parts, can become the means of earning a wage once more. The environment is reinterpreted by the men. Reinterpeting the environment continues throughout the film.

While the factory becomes a place for perfecting their routines, Gerald's 'respectable' home becomes a place for honing their bodies and their strength as a group. Gerald's home is a significant space in the film. The first time they go there Dave picks his way through Gerald's ornaments and at first Gerald is anxious that they should not touch his belongings. It appears to be a place of sanctity, where his respectability is still intact.

In the scene where they assemble at Gerald's home for the first attempt at taking their clothes off, Gerald worries that their actions will lower the tone of the area. Just as they are all down to their underwear and socks, bailiffs arrive to remove his symbols of respectability as he has not been able to keep up the payments on them. Their disrespectable costume is in absolute and comic contrast here to the respect and honour they show their friend in seeing off the bailiffs and allowing Gerald to continue to delude his wife that all is well. Where Gerald lives, his gnomes, his wife's health-and-fitness equipment all give us insight to the fabric of Gerald's life. The way we are shown his standing is through the mise-en-scène.

This principle applies to the way we are shown all of the other main character's lives. Gaz's home is modest, dimly lit, poorly furnished, appropriately indicative of his low standing in the world. His home is bleak and empty – Nathan complains that it is cold – and it is in direct contrast to his ex-wife's which is mock-Georgian, large and well preserved, brightly lit and reflecting her better, more comfortable standing in the world with her new partner.

For the most part the rehearsals take place in the factory and do move apace, but there is no mistaking that such a location represents danger and the dress rehearsals are interrupted by a policeman checking the 'legal' use of the building. The near perfect performance is captured on a security video suggesting that it is not licit activity and threatens to put paid to the whole thing. The men first see themselves 'dancing good' while under arrest in a police station. The mise-en-scène clearly suggests that they are acting outside the ordinary rules.

The mise-en-scène does function in different ways, however. The infamous dole office scene, for example, shows them perfecting their 'work' skills while waiting to sign on the dole again. There are many contrasts in the film between the desires or motivations of the men and the position that they find themselves in. The difficulty of their social position is constantly underscored by the mise-en-scène.

This contrast is finally brought out in the actual stripping scene that ends the film. The men bring together all of their rehearsal of roles in one final act. They wear the costumes of security guards as if in defiance of the only apparent work that is seen in the film (both Lomper and Dave are security guards at different times).

In the final scene these clothes are removed, a refusal to accept security jobs as proper labour, and the men are back in the working-men's club albeit in reversed role with a female clientele screaming for them to remove their clothes. Here, however, the mise-en-scène is correct – there are mirrorballs, bright lights and microphones, an enthusiastic audience and all the right accoutrements to make the men's reinvented roles as strippers work for them.

The camera properly focuses on their stripping. For the most part the camera has been quite static in the film, accordant with their own stasis. But here the camera swerves and moves and makes far greater use of camera angles. Jean screams as Dave tears his shirt off and the joy of women is made evident by the camera moving through the crowd capturing their elation. The men deliver their routine as best as they are able and the scene is identical to the one showing exuberant women screaming for The Chippendales at the beginning of the film.

The Full Monty is stylistically efficient while being unremarkable in terms of cinematography. It is a film grown from a long-standing genre of British films which are essentially about the drama of everyday life. The emphasis of this film is firmly in the script and quality of acting. The stylistic elements support key themes: the loss of traditional masculine identity; unemployment; loss of dignity. But the cinematography does not seek to draw the spectator's attention away from the core story and from the characters. It uses a standard episodic narrative, one event following another to a conclusion.

Like Loach, Cattaneo has made this film bring into view the lines on faces, the way the light falls in a room, how men walk down a street, where they live and what the fabric of life is like for men in the late 1990s.

social realism or comedy?

One of the ways in which this film clearly departs from the British New Wave style is its comedy. While elements of a film's style do contribute to elaborating a serious, political reading of the film, they also contribute to the film as comedy and this film was marketed as a comedy not as a piece of social realism.

The use of location, placing men in children's places brings about as much laughter as it does cause for contemplation. It is funny when Gaz and Dave are balanced on a car roof in the middle of a canal and when they use the gnome to discredit Gerald at his job interview, or when Dave nicks a sweet in the Asda pick'n'mix, or when the men are standing semi-naked in Gerald's house threatening the bailiffs to 'Put down and piss off'.

There is much humour in the fact that the men are in improbable locations throughout and that the mise-en-scène is entirely inappropriate to what is ordinarily an erotic act of stripping. Short of Reg's shame and inability to take his clothes off, most of the other men appear to embark on the stripping venture as if it is an entirely reasonable way of making money. Dave has his own personal doubts about appearing but is, at various turns, convinced that it is as likely a way as any of earning some cash.

The humour of the film derives from the diversity of men: different shapes, ages, sizes, colours and sexual orientation all make for a laugh at the men's expense. If the camera angles do a lot to draw attention to the men's dilemmas they also do a lot to draw attention towards the absurdity of this spectacle. The camera refuses to make any of the men particularly desirable. For the most part, the camera is static and stays at a distance to the men when they are rehearsing. The men are only ever semi-naked (until the final shot) and even then the shot of six distinctly different shaped men and their backsides leaves one laughing rather than sighing with desire.

When they first take their clothes off in Gerald's house, the camera swerves tellingly between one imperfection and the next: Dave's stomach, Lomper's pigeon chest and each and every different pair of underwear and socks! The sight of half naked men in a backdrop of a kitsch suburban home is anything but erotic.

The mise-en-scène in Gerald's house does foreground his handle on respectability and the need to retain his status but, at the same time, it also ensures that we see this respectability as something of a ridiculous façade in the light of his true position in the world. Suburban kitsch is to be mocked and it is mocked when, using the same mise-en-scène, the men bond over their poor physical shape in Gerald's wife's bedroom. Their understanding of the degradation of the stripping spectacle is brought to light as they tan on machines, sit on exercise bikes and worry about what women may say about them, especially if it's anything like what they say about women.

social realism or comedy? style

Later when Dave retreats to his potting shed we are expecting him to dwell on his weight worries or his impotence, but instead we see him eat a chocolate bar while wrapping himself in cling film. The improbability is ripe for humour.

Peter Cattaneo, the director, remarked in the foreword to Simon Beaufoy's script that 'Issues of male identity, gender roles, body politics and the effects of long-term unemployment are dealt with but without the script ever becoming didactic. These themes are always present but never at the expense of character or story'. The economical style permits character and story to be prominent, and for the serious themes to be present but not to detract from the comic elements of the story.

Close-ups are also used therefore at key comic moments: the most memorable lines are delivered in close-up, when Gaz asks Dave to 'borrow me' a jacket for the funeral and Dave asks the colour. Gaz remarks quite straight-faced 'orange'. Likewise Gaz is shot in mid close-up when watching his mates practice their dance steps in the dole queue. His expression of pleasure matches how we are to view the scene. While the use of a tight frame and close-up helps to elaborate the serious issues, equally these style elements help to keep the comic moments alive.

The film is stylistically efficient but it is not what stays in the viewer's mind necessarily. There are no blinding special effects or expressionistic lights. In keeping with the episodic narrative the film uses a style that brings a sharp script and keen acting out. It is a straightforward style appropriate for the kind of film it is intended to be.

film sound & music

The film was released with an accompanying soundtrack and the sound has a vital role to play in terms of the narrative (see Narrative and Form) and for enhancing both the social realism and humour. The film makes quite extensive use of a period soundtrack as atmosphere. The film is seeking to deal with the changes to the position of men over the past twenty-five years and the accompanying soundtrack refers back to that period: Hot Chocolate, Sister Sledge, Steve Harley and Cockney Rebel all had hits during the 1970s. The use of their lyrics is a reminder of how things used to be.

editing

The actual score of the film is various enough to assist certain emotional moments: the score lifts and fades dependent upon the feelings of the character it is accompanying. The wider soundtrack has both a narrative function (as discussed in the previous chapter) and has an emotional function highlighting the feelings and emotions of the characters. Playing 'You Sexy Thing' for the first time represents a key move towards realising the dream of putting together a strip troupe and is used to buoy their low self-esteem.

One of the happier moments of the film is given emphasis by the use of Steve Harley and Cockney Rebel's number 'Come Up And See Me, Make Me Smile', for a more joyous return to the outdoors and to activity involving a group rather than individuals. Using Tom Jones 'You Can Keep Your Hat On' enables the men to appropriate some of the sex appeal of Tom Jones and assists their final performance and journey towards self respect.

editing

In the chapter on narrative I referred to the fact that all narratives are compressed. The process of editing is, therefore, a vital aspect of style connecting one part of the narrative to the next. The principal shared feature of film narratives is that of realism, presenting a recognisable version of the world back to the audience. Editing contributes to the illusion that a story is unfolding naturally. Editing, in socially realist films such as *The Full Monty* appears seamless, invisible. The shots appear joined together to push a narrative forward in time toward a resolution. Two key editing techniques are the fade-out and the dissolve.

The Full Monty is shot episodically with most events referring forwards rather than back. Consequently the editing is a simple cut from one shot to the next. The skill, for the editor is to make this transition largely invisible – editing out on a motivation from one part of the action to its resolve in the next. In the first six scenes of the film this pattern of editing is established. The film opens with montage of two shots. Montage is essentially a means of mixing elements to give common associations or is used more commonly now to deal with a time delay. Hence the opening of

end motivation assisting the comprehension

the film shows in two shots what Sheffield has been like in the past and what it is like now – an economical method.

The editing then shifts into scenes being cut together with an end motivation assisting the comprehension of the next shot. This is achieved often through dialogue or music. The first scene, the promotional film of success, is contrasted with the second by the sounds of steel being dragged along the floor. The second scene is cut to the third through a sound cue – brass band music linked to the shot of the band. The third scene is linked to the fourth via a dialogue cue: 'Shut up, I'm thinking' remarks Gaz as they are locked into the factory and the fourth shot reveals a ropey plan of escape balanced on a car in the canal. Motivations from one shot establish the relevance of the next.

The speed, pace and rhythm of editing is important, too. *The Full Monty* is edited at a constant speed in keeping with the slow unfolding of ideas, and setbacks. Social-realist films tend to stay within a strict rhythm of shots in order to maintain attention on character and action, rather than effect. Outside of the final sequence when the men are shot from many different angles and the sequence cut together more quickly, the film maintains a steady pace in keeping with the themes.

conclusion

In the process of analysing a film it is possible to isolate certain features of style and to contemplate how these work together to produce the meanings of the film. Most people do not purchase a ticket to the cinema with the express purpose of unravelling the ways in which narrative and style are working in the film. Yet our pleasure in a film depends upon whether we agree with the conventions of representation offered in the style. Whether we are a film analyst or a member of the viewing public, we are all actively trying to interpret the codes of a film in order to make sense of it. This chapter has outlined the ways in which aspects of style affect the 'reading' of a film. The question of active spectatorship is taken up more formally in the next chapter, Contexts.

contexts

In the previous section *The Full Monty* was compared stylistically to films from the British New Wave (see Style) and to more contemporary expressions of social realism, for example the work of Ken Loach. These comparisons will be developed further in this chapter in the sections on Intertextuality and Genre. The first section of this chapter, however, is more concerned with the ideological context of *The Full Monty* and what the film offers in terms of different representations of masculinity.

The Full Monty was produced at a pivotal point in British history. After eighteen years of Conservative rule, during which work had been extensively restructured, Britain stood poised for a change in government – New Labour. In New Labour's rhetoric was the word 'modernisation' and a need to respond to a Britain based on new technology and commerce rather than on manufacture. Implicit in this rhetoric was the need for people to re-train, re-think and re-order their lives according to this new world order.

The Full Monty does not seek to resurrect debates about the steel industry necessarily. The producer, Uberto Pasolini, said that he was not interested in the film being a diatribe on politics or the Thatcher effect in Britain. The film does not seek to offer wide reaching conclusions on what should happen to men. It does not pose arguments for the reintroduction of the manufacturing industry. The dialogue of the men shows both depression and resignation to the fact that their old working life has gone. The film takes up the personal side of the effects of the decline of manufacturing industry: what happens to men when traditional industry no longer needs them? In this way it is a New Labour kind of film and indeed the film was warmly received by Tony Blair and given an even higher profile when Prince Charles visited the set and mimicked the scene in the dole office.

If the broader picture of British life is removed from the film then the attention that it draws to other values is what needs to be discussed here. The film takes the issue of contemporary masculinity as a key theme. It seeks to explore, through comedy, what men may need to do to recover their self-esteem and worth.

representation & stereotypes

Representation is one of the key concepts of Film and Media Studies. Essentially the discussion of representation enables the viewer to ask questions about how certain media texts present the world as we know it back to us. Studying representation reminds us of how we are given information and ideas about the world. It is a 'political' term in that it enables us to study the ways in which certain ideas and values are either restricted or opened up for wider intereptation.

A central area of debate about ideology – the sets of values offered by the media – has been focused around representation and stereotypes. The term stereotype means that the producers of texts reduce the characteristics of a diverse group of people to a few recognisable ideas.

The Full Monty does seek to offer quite a wide range of representations of men. The stripping troupe is formed from two friends, their old manager (say, ten years their senior), Horse who is argued as 'fifty if he's a day' and two younger men: Lomper and Guy. The diversity of representation does, in the first instance, ensure very different audience responses to male unemployment as each and every character has a different personal story. All of the men are working class – each refers to a life at 'Harrisons' when it was open. However, the film seeks to differentiate working-class experience via the different identities and values of each of the characters. Gaz appears initially to represent a common stereotype of the working-class man holding on to traditional ideas of the roles of men and women. He is horrified at seeing women in the men's club and even more so in the men's toilets when one of the women stands and urinates like a man. Dave's values offer a balance to these ideas. He constantly reminds Gaz

what kind of view ... is being offered

that 'Jean would' spend her money to see men strip and implicitly supports her to use her money in a way she sees fit.

The differentiation of working-class experience is further made by offering specific representations of race and sexuality. One of the more interesting representations on offer is that of Horse. In the first instance this working-class existence has a history of being displayed as a white existence. The film conforms with this representation in offering a majority white cast. However, the use of a black character does assist in the belief that black workers were engaged in this life, too, and is a significant departure from the more recognisable uses of black characters in a range of other dramas.

In considering the use of stereotypes it is important to ask questions about what kind of view of a certain group of people is being offered. Within the dialogue and the plot there is an explicit attempt to challenge a common stereotype about black men: that they are sexually potent. Horse indeed adopts this stereotype for himself when trying to forge his way into the troupe. He is 'uncovered' later when they first take their clothes off.

This stereotype of the black man is challenged implicitly and explicitly. At the first meeting with Horse, Lomper shows his ignorance of the stereotype by nudging Gaz to ask why Horse is called 'Horse'. Later Dave tests Jean's response to the stereotype by asking her if she would consider going out with a black man, and interprets her response as an affirmation of black male sexual prowess. She undercuts this by arguing that only 'some of them' have got great bodies as if to assert that it is only the same as arguing that 'some' white men do.

The only dilemma the film focuses on as Horse's is his concern over the size of his 'wanger' with one close-up of him in a phone box trying to figure out the directions for using a penis enlarger. The film therefore refutes the use of a black stereotype and seeks to bring black experience of unemployment in line with white experience. Horse speaks like a northerner, dresses and appears as the other men and his life, outside of the one worry about sexual potency, is reduced to a similar life of the men. If this is a good refutation of a use of black stereotypes, it might also be argued that the film elides a direct representation of the specific problems that black men may have gaining work. There is no explicit mention of either personal or structural racism in the film.

The majority of men are heterosexual and their motivation to strip is based on a reversal of the traditional male/female roles in attracting sexual interest. Another minor aspect of the plot is the developing relationship between Lomper and Guy brought to realisation when they escape from arrest and tumble into Lomper's bedroom. At one level it is an attempt to suggest – positively – that there are gay men among the working classes who are only differentiated from their comrades via their choice of sexual partner.

Guy and Lomper's sexuality is not signalled by different clothing or by a characteristic walk or gesture or use of catch-phrases – all stereotypical ways of categorising gay men. Their essentially private choice of sexual partner is brought into view by extracting them from the group and placing them in a private situation in Lomper's bedroom. The idea is cemented further at the funeral when they are seen holding hands, but little is made of this by the other characters outside of Dave's wry remark at the funeral that there is 'nowt as queer as folk'.

While different representations are on offer, the film tends to skirt over the differences and bring the men back to the same base line. The men themselves seem to demonstrate little in the way of prejudice towards each other or more broadly. Ideologically this is potentially quite subversive as it does seem to suggest that the more unifying elements of human experience – in this instance unemployment – supersede the marginal differences between them.

The lack of prejudice shown and the attempt to 'normalise' the black and gay experience within the wider experience does reflect a shift in values in the wider society in 1997. The men are far more united by their position in the world – all unemployed men – than by the personal/political differences which might divide them. It is an optimistic approach to the ways in which ethnic minorities and gay groups have been accepted into mainstream views. Although, it is also a deliberate attempt not to tackle wider issues or make the film a discussion of 1990s politics writ large. There have been gradual moves within the law and social policy to bring about equality for various groups within society. The film reflects those kinds of liberal discourses about equality. But recent events – bombings in Brixton, Brick Lane and Soho – still suggest that racism and homophobia are clearly felt within the wider world. For better or worse, *The Full Monty* does not seek to make racism or homophobia areas of concern or debate.

genre & cultural context

Genre is a French term which is used in the context of film to refer to the way films may be categorised according to shared characteristics. The study of genre enables the analyst to examine any one film in the context of others with which it shares similar features. In Narrative and Form it was suggested that the audience becomes aware of particular conventions for telling a story and it is this awareness of familiar elements that assists both comprehension and pleasure. The way the narrative conjoins with certain features of style will usually ensure that the audience expectation is set for the genre.

Genre has a function, therefore, in helping the viewer to solve a film's enigmas. It is a clear way of signalling what kind of story the viewer should expect. Making films according to generic conventions has a wider function than assisting audience expectation. The financial success of films actually depends to some extent on meeting audience expectation. Genre is an economic as well as a cultural function. When films share like characteristics they can attract similar marketing and use their familiarity to attract similar audiences.

Marketing of films is usually conducted on the basis of both genre and stars. The clearest example of this process at work was in the hey-day of the Hollywood Studio System. Between the 1930s and 1950s film studios divided their output according to genre. Within the vertically integrated structure of production, distribution and exhibition different studios became highly proficient at producing particular genres of films. Some critics have argued that such emphasis on film craft brought about some of the best films of the twentieth century. Other critics have argued the opposite, that the manufacture of films according to strict generic conventions destroyed creativity and innovation and restricted the range of stories that might be told in film.

While repetition of elements is undoubtedly important for signalling the kind of film the audience is watching, there is also a need to exhibit variation. Street (1997:106) groups many 1980s–90s films into a genre she describes as 'hybrid': 'issue-based films that encompass several generic elements from comedy to thriller'. These hybrid films, she argues, set up dilemmas but refuse to offer solutions. The low production values of *The Full Monty* makes it recognisable as a British film in a socially realist tradition (see Style). In this respect the use of location, choice of actors and core theme of unemployment have it conforming to that tradition. But it is also a significant departure from that tradition. For one, this is a comedy – most films in this genre are melodramatic rather than comedic.

intertextuality

The comedy is reinforced through the range of intertextual references. Intertextuality is a term that refers to the other texts referenced by a film. This aspect of genre assists the audience in their expectations. The themes of unemployment, decline of manufacturing industry and position of men in the late twentieth century are all subjects that have been in evidence in British films and TV drama in the 1980s and 1990s.

The most recent film that *The Full Monty* refers to implicitly is *Brassed Off* (1996, dir. Mark Herman). This film, also set in the North, deals with the decline of the coal industry through the ways in which a connected pursuit – brass band playing – is affected. Also played by an ensemble cast it takes up the importance of playing in a band and the continuous need for the pride such competition brings.

While *Brassed Off* offers humour through the characterisation, it also operates in the more gritty tradition of social realism in exposing the extent of poverty and demise for the abandoned pit community. Like *The Full Monty*, however, it only offers a solution to the immediate crisis rather than posing any wider agenda. It has a very similar closure – the pit band playing at The Royal Albert Hall in a competition and winning its immediate pride back again.

In 1991 Ken Loach's *Riff Raff* was released. *Riff Raff* was about the lives of itinerant workers on a building site. This film also took up the issue of how men who had been previously employed as a work force manoeuvred themselves into new conditions of work. The irony of the film – intended to be a comment on the state of Britain at that time – was that the only new work on offer appeared to be building luxury flats from sold-off State assets, a hospital.

In the 1980s Alan Bleasdale's acclaimed television drama *Boys from the Blackstuff* showed a group of northern men trying to carve out a new life from the debris of the old. Some of the men gained work on a building site and ironically discovered that their work was to create a dole office. This was a drama about men being defeated by the change in working life. It showed marital breakdown, descent into criminality, loss of children to the State and mental illness. While there was much humour, the torment of unemployment took precedence.

The Full Monty – a film about male unemployment – refers back to these kinds of texts and in the first instance might establish expectations for the audience to view the film as a kitchen-sink drama in the old tradition. But while these references are there, the film also offers new references. The use of *Flashdance*, for example, helps to put expectations in a different direction. In this popular hit of the 1980s, a female welder works to establish her dream of becoming a dancer.

This reference is vital for two reasons: one it reflects the men's own position – the clip from *Flashdance* references manufacturing industry, Jenifer Gray is a welder. But it also references another way of making her dreams come true – dancing. Dave complains about *Flashdance*'s lack of realism with respect to welding but this only seems to reinforce the other's feelings that there is a need to re-think their role in the world. It doesn't matter after all whether Dave could be a better welder, that option is not on offer, he does however have an option to learn to dance.

While *Riff Raff, Brassed Off, Boys from the Blackstuff* all handle male unemployment specifically and with a great deal of sobriety and political purpose, *The Full Monty* turns the genre in a new direction to examine the more optimistic and resourceful ways in which men in the 1990s handle their plight.

STARS

The recognition of common conventions is a vital aspect of genre. Likewise the use of stars has an intertextual dimension. The ways in which the audience knows the star from other texts assists the reading and understanding of the film role. The use of a recognised star can assist in

Robert Carlyle

the function of the narrative. But like genre, the use of the star also has an economic function. Audience identification with and/or admiration for a star can be a vital element in whether people will go to the cinema to see the film. Thus the use of stars has both a narrative and economic function.

The British New Wave of cinema in the 1960s sought to construct a heroic working-class figure by moving away from the use of stars. The directors

intertextuality

of such films believed that the audience should recognise the character before the star. The hero's typicality – a representative figure of other men like him – was foregrounded over any exceptional qualities.

The Full Monty does not rebuke the star system entirely. Instead the choice to use Robert Carlyle coincided with the particular feel of the

Paul Barber   Hugo Speer

film they wanted to create. Robert Carlyle is a perfect amalgam of star and character. By 1997 he was a well-recognised figure of British cinema (*Riff Raff, Trainspotting, Face*) and of the small screen (*Cracker, Hamish MacBeth*). In each of these roles he plays variously a man on the border of licit/illicit activity. The character of Gaz fits this history of Carlyle on the screen. Carlyle represents a popular figure of British cinema acting and his repertoire of characters is in keeping with the character he plays here. Using Carlyle in the role of Gaz helps the viewer to quickly comprehend the kind of character he is. But the film is also able to use Carlyle's previous accomplishments as a way of marketing the film (see

representative of ordinary folk

Marketing Success). Carlyle has starred in films made by Ken Loach. There is some intertextual value here, Loach's films have a sharp, political agenda usually and recognising Carlyle from these texts gives *Monty* a political edge, too.

The rest of the ensemble is played by relatively unknown actors. Paul Barber (Horse) is a recognisable support actor from the hit BBC sit-com *Only Fools and Horses* where his association with Del Boy and Rodney has him cemented in the mind of the audience as a character on the fringe of

Lomper, Dave, Guy and Horse

things. Barber also briefly played a role of a fringe-villain in *Brookside* and had a cameo role in Antonia Bird's film *Priest* also starring Tom Wilkinson (Gerald).

Mark Addy (Dave), Steve Huison (Lomper) and Hugo Speer (Guy) are all relatively new screen faces. The use of the relatively unknown actors is both an economic and aesthetic decision. In keeping with the social realist function of casting, the actors' lack of previous exposure assists

production history

the viewer reading the characters as representative of ordinary folk. But it is important to remember that the film was made on a very low budget (£2.2m) and, therefore, would have had little flexible room for a celebrity cast.

production history

The Full Monty was a low-budget comedy (costing only £2.2m to make) and went on general release in Britain on 29 August 1997. At the end of that week Diana, Princess of Wales died in a car crash. In the first weekend, the period of Princess Diana's funeral, over 1.8 million people saw the film. The film recovered its little budget in box-office returns on the first weekend of release in Britain. It competed admirably with a whole array of Hollywood blockbusters (see Screen International UK Top 15 Chart).

UK TOP 15

Rank		Film / Origin / Distributor	Week	Three-day gross Sept 5–7	Screens Sept 7	Screen Average	Three-day % change	Total gross to Sept 7
1	(2)	THE FULL MONTY (UK) 20th Century Fox	2	$2,528,109	226	$11,186	+1	$7,374,530
2	(-)	AUSTIN POWERS (US) Pathe Distribution	NEW	$1,543,460	266	$5,802	–	$1,543,460
3	(1)	MEN IN BLACK (US) Columbia Tristar	6	$1,416,910	350	$4,049	-48	$50,661,321
4	(3)	BEAN (UK) Polygram	5	$1,009,953	391	$2,582	-53	$23,430,640
5	(4)	CONSPIRACY THEORY (US) Warner Bros	2	$819,704	338	$2,426	-56	$3,481,277
6	(5)	EVENT HORIZON (US) UIP	3	$495,302	186	$2,663	-41	$4,223,824
7	(-)	MRS BROWN (UK) BVI	NEW	$361,502	149	$2,426	–	$361,502
8	(6)	THE LOST WORLD: JURASSIC PARK (US) UIP	8	$231,989	188	$1,234	-57	$39,310,137
9	(7)	SPEED 2: CRUISE CONTROL (US) 20th Century Fox	4	$191,008	169	$2,679	-61	$5,401,297
10	(8)	ROMY AND MICHELE'S ... REUNION (US) BVI	3	$179,614	124	$1,448	-50	$1,982,992
11	(-)	NIGHT FALLS ON MANHATTAN (US) First Independent	NEW	$139,690	111	$1,258	–	$139,690
12	(10)	GROSSE POINTE BLANK (US) BVI	5	$55,196	37	$1,492	-47	$1,453,437
13	(9)	LADY AND THE TRAMP (US) BVI	11	$40,036	185	$217	-71	$3,401,483
14	(11)	LOST HIGHWAY (US) Polygram	3	$37,283	20	$1,864	-40	$294,668
15	(-)	L'APPARTEMENT (Fr) Artificial Eye	NEW	$18,434	1	$18,434	–	$18,434

© *Screen International*

INDUSTRIAL CONTEXT

Film producers, directors and actors have all argued for the need to sustain a national cinema, one which reflects the diversity and vibrancy of British life. Indeed it is only a national cinema that is capable of responding to the more fluid sense of cultural identity in Britain. British cinema has offered interpretations of 'Englishness' (for example, the 'heritage cinema' genre, grown from original novels like *A Room with a View* or *Howards End*). But it has also offered, as evidenced by the popularity of Danny Boyle's films *Shallow Grave* (1994) and *Trainspotting* (1996), representations of life from the Celtic borders.

Attracting finance for 'national' rather than international projects has been very difficult and is made more so by the fact that Hollywood dominates production, distribution and exhibition of films within America and globally. Preserving a national cinema has been argued for on the grounds of its contribution to cultural identity. National cinema is not intended to compete necessarily with the global success of Hollywood productions but to complement that output, as part of preserving diversity. Economic realities – the uncertain success of British national cinema abroad – has left producers struggling, often unsuccessfully, to raise funds for specifically British stories. The imperative to make a box-office profit has too often prevented independent producers gaining the chance to extend the national cinema project.

The relationship between production, distribution and exhibition is considered broadly in the next section and then applied specifically to the unusual production history of *The Full Monty*.

Before a film is made, a series of production decisions have to take place. These are largely to do with raising funds and making a successful project. The bid for funds can have a profound effect on the look and style of a film. In Hollywood this frequently entails a battle over stars and directors. It may also entail considerable revisions to original screenplays and to the quality of direction. This has sometimes led to critics charging Hollywood with repeating the same old stories (see genre). In Britain the pre-production procedure has less effect on the content of the film quite simply because there are very few funders to apply to. More likely is the fact that an idea,

production history

good or bad, cannot very readily get off the ground.

Within the pre-production phase, various negotiations need to take place regarding the extent of distribution and the means of exhibition. The distribution process refers to advertising and marketing, the process of 'selling' the film to audiences. Exhibition refers to where and how a film is seen. For American film production these processes are often handled within the same company. Paramount, Warners, Fox and Disney remain key players in Hollywood film production but their real power lies in their control over distribution and exhibition.

A key institutional battle in the 1980s was played out in Britain with the loss of smaller cinemas to the multiplexes, cinema complexes with many screens. Ownership of a multiplex necessitates mass audiences for films and it has been a key problem for British film-makers trying to ensure exhibition for their films. If the film appears to have minority interest then it can be difficult to ensure it will get booked into a screen at a multiplex. If a film cannot be exhibited then it cannot recover its costs, let alone make a profit. For British films this has an effect on the development of a national cinema. Can it ever be more than 'one-off' success?

The Full Monty is listed as a British film. It has a British director, scriptwriter and cast. It has an Italian producer (who has worked within the British film industry). Yet the film was funded by an American Distributor – Fox Searchlight. The particular production context of *The Full Monty* is an interesting one.

It was Uberto Pasolini (see Background, Biographies), the producer, who had the idea for the film. It was a raw idea 'unemployed men turn to stripping to raise cash'. He first approached Simon Beaufoy to write a script. Pasolini approached Film on Four which funded the development of the script and was interested in a co-production. Pasolini had to find partner funders. He had other contacts in the film industry and drew on his experience. He approached Lindsay Law who was working in 20th Century Fox running the Fox Searchlight division. This division dealt with low budget art-house films. Pasolini showed Law the script and secured all the money from Fox. Gaining the support of 20th Century Fox was a vital factor in the success of *The Full Monty*.

PROS AND CONS FOR AN AMERICAN DISTRIBUTOR

For 20th Century Fox, the advantages were extensive. Fox knew it was able to cover the risks by using its prime position in the industry to gain exhibition rights in the US and ensure a mass American audience. Secondly, Fox has links with Rupert Murdoch's other interests, Sky Television. The moment it agreed to back the film, it secured rights for the film to be shown first on satellite.

For Pasolini and the rest of the team the advantages of a single American backer were also extensive. The film would most obviously benefit from a well-oiled distribution strategy. It would be marketed on a par with other American releases. This process began early when Fox Searchlight screened the film at the Sundance Film Festival in Utah in January 1997. The Sundance Festival has a reputation for screening new talent and for putting marginal films into mainstream reviews.

In the first wave of newspaper reviews, the film was triumphed as a feel-good movie with something for everyone. It was only later when other commentators began to ask questions about the way in which the film had received a truly American rather than British opening that Emma Forrest of the *Guardian* mused that 'it took a US company to get a British film properly released in Britain' (27.10.97 *Guardian*).

Marketing considerations can impinge on the construction of a film, guiding important creative and production decisions. When Pasolini approached Fox Searchlight the go-ahead was given on the basis of the reputations of those involved in the production. Lindsay Law liked Cattaneo's work for television. He trusted Pasolini and unusually did not insist that any major stars should be included to boost interest in the film. Fox Searchlight backed out of the creative decisions and focused all their energies on distribution and exhibition.

The Full Monty is a film that had the liberty to develop an idea with the extraordinary financial backing of a major American distributor and which, unusually, did not have to compromise the artistic content.

The danger, for many critics of American intervention in British film-making is that there will be a drive towards a Hollywood-isation of British film. Perhaps *Four Weddings and a Funeral* and more recently its

marketing success

companion film *Notting Hill* (1999) are examples of that cross over. Must Hugh Grant and a major Hollywood star (Andie McDowell or Julia Roberts) always be the recipe for transatlantic success? Will British national identity be diluted in a quest to reproduce American versions of England for an American audience? *The Full Monty* production context would seem to refute that, but the questions such a co-production raises nevertheless remain unanswered.

marketing success

Once the film had been made, Fox Searchlight set about the release of the film. It was first shown in America, two weeks before being released in Britain, and the showing took place amid tough competition. *GI Jane* starring one of the most bankable stars in Hollywood – Demi Moore – was on release as was *Men in Black* sporting 40 million dollars worth of special effects. *The Full Monty* could not compete in terms of star or special effects. But Fox Searchlight's marketing strategy began early with the intention of as many people as possible seeing it before it was released. This strategy was to create a 'word-of-mouth' interest in the film. Then it used its considerable prowess in the American marketplace to ensure the film was booked into multiplexes and backed by a massive publicity campaign. This campaign was then transferred to Britain.

There are a range of publicity tools available to the distributor and it is clear from the volume of publicity available that *The Full Monty* was given a lot of backing. In the first instance there was a pre-release strategy, teaser campaign through trailers in cinemas, billboard adverts establishing the title of the film in the audience's mind. Much was made of the humour and the title: *The Full Monty* was to pass into common parlance. The fact that the film made extensive use of a sountrack opened the publicity outlets to music stores (advertising the accompanying CD) and to radio where many of the songs gained air-play.

Upon release there were newspaper reviews (see over). Creating a positive response has a bearing on audience figures, equally, though, newspapers and magazines ran a range of articles about the various characters and actors. There were interviews with Robert Carlyle and articles about him that ran across the quality press and in women's magazines. Mark Addy (Dave) was interviewed by the men's magazine *Loaded*. Further articles appeared on Tom Wilkinson (Gerald) and Paul Barber (Horse) in the press and TV listings magazines. The continuation of interest in the film was sustained through the actors and the title remaining constantly in the public eye.

Advertising and interviews are effective ways of drawing attention to a film. But there are other strategies that keep up the momentum of a campaign. *The New Statesman* reported that a website on *The Full Monty* had been established to generate interest in the month before the release. 'Surfers' of the net were invited to send pictures of themselves to the web site with their private parts covered. There was to be a first prize of an 18–30s holiday to Ibiza as a reward for the most interesting and novel picture. Such interest for the 'idea' was continued with various merchandising tie-ins – jeans, beer, underwear to name but a few.

A successful marketing campaign for a film will ensure that the audience wishes to be part of a whole experience of the film. The marketing phenomenon of *The Full Monty* way exceeded its critical reception. While it can be argued to be a 'feelgood' film, it did not set out to be a remarkable film and yet its success at the box office, backed by this wide-reaching marketing campaign, ensured that it has a legendary status as a successful British film. This success was rewarded recently when it was nominated number 26 in the list of top 100 British films this century (BFI).

There is clearly a relationship between a film's success and marketing. Yet as the critical responses that follow will illustrate, marketing is unlikely to be able to make a 'bad film' good. There are plenty of examples of Hollywood films with famous stars and directors that have flopped, despite the marketing. A film must work, it must have coherence and appeal and it must be able to please a fickle audience.

The marketing strategy for *The Full Monty* undoubtedly assisted a small, low-budget and distinctly British film to become an international success. Some critics have remarked that the superior work of the British Director, Mike Leigh (*Secrets and Lies*, 1997, a case in point) might have made a more significant impact if it had had the benefit of such strategies. This blanket offering of entertainment

would seem to suggest that while bad films cannot be made 'good' by marketing, 'good' films can fail to be successful, without it.

audience theory

The previous section about the marketing of the film demonstrates just how important it is for the distributors of a film to have a clear idea about audience. They thought *The Full Monty* was more likely to appeal to women than to men, and more likely to appeal to younger than to older people. However, the box office returns suggest that the film was viewed by more than the anticipated groups. A film about male stripping would appear to imply that the target audience is women but as the film puts far less emphasis on the sexual and more upon the comic, this focus invites a wider reading.

Within film and media studies there have been a range of different attempts to theorise the audience. While television audiences have been the object of frequent investigation in recent years, film audiences have been under-investigated.

The first analyses of the film audience were based on the study of film producing institutions – Hollywood. Mass communication research in the 1940s, epitomised by the work of the Frankfurt School, was essentially about how the mass media (and here this was mostly film) could influence the beliefs of the mass audiences. The analysis was not of audiences but of institutions, and the arguments proffered were that the Hollywood studios had considerable power to promote (what the theorists saw as) a bland cultural product for a mass audience.

In this blanket offering of entertainment it was argued that the producers of media had the power to create texts that kept audiences happy and prevented them asking awkward questions about society. Audiences were not investigated by these theorists, instead the perception of audiences was grown from analysis of media industrial practice and from the presumption about the low quality of the product.

audience theory

SPECTATORSHIP THEORY

In the 1960s and 1970s new theories were formed about the audience specifically with respect, to reading film. Spectatorship theory was concerned with textual analysis and textual constructs. It drew on psychoanalysis as a method of thinking about how audiences were invited to view texts, and how this subconscious practice of viewing fed into an uncritical support for establishment values. This theoretical viewpoint also did not entail any audience research. Industrial practice and close textual reading were combined to argue what the imagined specator's reading of the text was.

In 1975 Laura Mulvey published an article entitled 'Visual Pleasure and Narrative Cinema' (see Bibliography). In this article Mulvey argued that film, and theatre, reflects on socially established interpretations of sexual differences which control images, erotic ways of looking and spectacle. She charged that the practices of Hollywood cinema invited spectators to view women in a way that ensured their continued subjugation to men. Mulvey reasoned that this happened because there was a well established code of spectatorship where women were presented as sexual spectacle both as objects of pleasure for the characters within the narrative and for the spectator in the auditorium. She argued that ways of looking (and this was combined with ways of interpreting or understanding) were constructed in three ways:

■ by the camera man and production team in establishment and framing of a shot

■ by the look within the film 'male characters objectify the female ones through their active, desiring and powerful "look" '

■ by the way the spectator's gaze is constructed through the above mechanisms

Mulvey argued that this process of film-making contributed significantly to the ways in which women were viewed in society: as sexual objects for male pleasure and satisfaction. She went on to point out that women would have to fight against this mechanism by creating their own style of film-making that was less predicated on pleasure than on progressive ideas of looking.

Needless to say there has been much critical response to Mulvey's point of view. Some feminist commentators took Mulvey's comments and developed them to argue that women in modern cinema are always seen as objects of sexual desire, the emphasis is still on women's bodies and not on men's. Mulvey reasoned that women could never look at men, like men look at women. She said that the image of women in film is always centred, it is always prominent and there to draw external spectator's interest to a film. Critics against Mulvey have said that increasingly men are appearing in film as objects of desire and while it is far from an equal arrangement (women do take their clothes off more than men) there is growing evidence to suggest that women spectators want to see men offered up for sexual desire.

CONSTRUCTING THE SPECTATOR'S GAZE

The first part of Mulvey's argument is that the production process actually sets up how the spectator will view a film. It is how a shot is established and framed.

In *The Full Monty* the first attempt to establish a group of men who will strip takes place in the factory. Each man's rehearsal efforts are given in medium long-shot. This is intended to have a particular effect. In the first place it demonstrates the men's own embarassment with what they are doing, their own distance from the practice and, secondly, it is also at the correct distance from the 'gaze' of the panel: Gaz, Dave, Gerald and Nathan. What is going on in these rehearsals is that a group of men are judging the sexual potential of other men. Men do not ordinarily look at men in this way unless the motive is sexual. As the panel do not hold this as an explicit motive there is evidence in the camera work (the medium long-shot) to show them keeping a distance from the gaze.

Mulvey's second level of analysis was that 'male characters objectify the female ones through their active, desiring and powerful look'. In this process the spectator's gaze is constructed. If male characters within the narrative cannot look at each other with an 'active, desiring and powerful look' then, according to Mulvey's thesis, it is not possible for the external spectator or audience to look at these men in that way. Arguably a film that is about male stripping is not objectifying men and holding them up to a female gaze. While the men do not give each other 'active and desiring looks' the female audience at the end does.

There are, of course, other scenes where this gaze is constructed rather differently. In the scene in Gerald's house, for example, the action necessitates a gaze. Gaz insists that they remove their clothes to rehearse the process of being looked at. The men do indeed look at each other, but any possible sexual content is undercut with the dialogue. Lomper is accused of having 'saggy tits' by Guy, and Gerald reassures Dave of the problem with his stomach with the line 'Fat is a feminist issue'. All the men remove their clothes without grace and stand in an array of underwear and socks that has the external spectator's eyes moving across the screen trying to make sense of the various different male shapes. Mulvey states that women's bodies are always 'centred' and therefore held up for gazing at. The diversity of masculinity here is far from centred and does prevent a fixed gaze at the male body.

Nevertheless one of the central problems with the men's rehearsals is the fact that they are not being 'looked at'. Gaz remarks very early on in the film when he does his strip in front of the car headlights that he 'needs an audience' to make it happen. Later the dress rehearsals are seen by Horse's family. These women still do not quite provide the right kind of gaze. Two of his aunties sit rather straight faced throughout the performance, one with her knitting, suggesting there is little in the performance to get excited about. Only his niece Beryl provides a little more youthful glamour.

It takes the men the whole film to rehearse an act that is worthy of female gaze. In the final sequence the strip is appropriately established and framed. The camera angles are significantly different here to any other point in the film – a lot of use of close-ups on the men's faces and actions. The camera, which has been static for much of the film, now moves and shoots Dave from below as he removes his shirt. The angle gives him height and power and as the camera rests on his stomach actually makes the act more sexual. At the moment Dave removes his shirt, Jean screams in approval. The male characters could now be seen to be 'objectified' by the 'active, desiring and powerful look' of the female audience in the film. At this moment, and only at this moment, could it be argued that the spectator's gaze is constructed as a sexual one. The exuberant female audience, screaming in approval at each new turn, brings the previously passive and unsmiling men into active and appreciative participants.

In the final analysis there are still things to be said about looking at men. The censorship rules in this country means that no shots of full frontal nudity are allowed. If one considers for a moment just how often and how much female nudity is permitted in films and indeed how important that objectification is to the marketability of a film, then this rather minor attempt at making men sexually desirable bears no comparison.

Using Mulvey's thesis I have tried to show how it is far from easy to look at men in the ways that an audience is used to looking at women and in this sense my analysis supports Mulvey's ideas. Dave replies to Jean's accusation that he might be having an affair with the line 'It's nowt to do with any fucking women, all right?' and it does seem to lend support to Mulvey's idea that women do not look at men like men look at women. The 'gaze' that the film constructs appears to be far more to do with recovering respect than it does with turning women on.

However, this is but one reading of the film. The distributors felt the 'hen night' audience would be an important one for the film. Getting women to scream in tandem with the audience within the film was a crucial part of its success. But it is perfectly possible that the film will be read differently by a male audience. Some parts of the audience will refuse a sexual reading of the film at all and see it entirely as a comedy. Others will wish to maintain the social and political dimensions of the film as well as its comedy. The social context in which the film is exhibited: a hen night or a late-night showing at an art-house cinema would probably generate different readings of the film.

Spectatorship theory enables the analyst to deconstruct images and conventions and to theorise how certain representations may be viewed and understood. The emphasis on textual analysis is a valuable one, but spectatorship theory does not allow for the possibility that audiences may read the same text in different ways.

SOCIAL AUDIENCE

In the immediate post-war period and in response to the introduction of television, specifically in America, audience research began to develop in different directions. There was still a strong emphasis on the fear of 'effects' from the media as epitomised by approaches in experimental psychology in America in the 1950s and 1960s where attempts were made to document how certain media texts made people think or behave.

Within the sociological tradition very different arguments were made. It was still broadly believed that the media had effects on people and that it was an important project to account for how and why the media has these effects. However, it was also argued that such effects are mediated by social and individual variables.

This 'uses and gratifications' approach essentially explored the idea that media could only have the effect the audience wanted from it. If the information given in a media text, for example, enhanced one's knowledge then it would have an 'effect'. If, however, such information was in contravention to already cherished values held by the audience then the message was unlikely to have any effect. The uses and gratifications approach supported ideas of differentiating the audience and acknowledging the vastly different social, economic, historical, gender, ethnic and personal experience the audience brings to the reading of a text. It also implied that knowing the audience depended upon researching and analysing the audience.

Instead of a mass audience, there were various moves in audience research to account for different readings and responses to the media. This tradition has grown and developed in the 1980s with studies that seek to understand text and audience simultaneously. In examining the text there is an attempt to understand what kind of 'preferred' readings are offered through the representation in a film. In then analysing the audience there is an attempt to understand the extent to which audiences may absorb, challenge or negotiate the meanings proposed by the text.

This tradition in audience research seeks to suggest that an audience watching media does not derive meaning and pleasure exclusively from the text. Some of the meanings and pleasures come about from the circumstances in which the text was consumed. In the instance of *The Full Monty*, any research about audience understanding of the film would have to take place within the context of examining the effects of the marketing strategy, the expectations created by the film, where it was viewed and who with.

The ways in which the cinema audience has been theorised and researched has been through a great deal of change. In the 1940s and in response to the prominence of Hollywood as a global medium, all theories of audience tended to be reduced to a mass audience idea. Spectatorship theory drew on the Mass Communication Theory, but drew attention to how texts work and joined those ideas with psychoanalytic approaches to reading and viewing. In the 1980s and 1990s researchers used a range of other methods to investigate audience pleasure and audience identification with the media, to account for the importance of the social as well as the textual in deriving meaning and pleasure from a text.

critical responses

In Britain *The Full Monty* was greeted with generous newspaper reviews. Newspaper criticism is a vital form of evaluation of a film and can have a great deal of influence on whether the film continues its success or failure from the opening impressions. Gaining 'a good review' is indeed a key part of the marketing strategy. The film was released on 29 August 1997 in Britain and in that first weekend over 1.6 million people saw it.

Prior to the actual release, Alexander Walker of the London *Evening Standard* reviewed the film, seriously remarking that '*The Full Monty* ... comes closest of all the films made in Britain in recent years in showing the way worklessness saps the will, disrupts the home, depresses the self-esteem'. This review set a tone for subsequent newspaper reviews although there is a clear divide in the reviews as to whether the film is primarily a comedy, or has something more serious to say about masculinity and unemployment.

The Sun's critic Nick Fisher (29.8.97) reviewed the film as being 'deliciously funny British bare-cheeked comedy, beautifully written for a cast that fits like a skin-tight g-string. It's funky, funny and feel-good without being naff'. *The Sun* has a significant readership – over three million usually – and the emphasis in Fisher's review on the sexual cheek of the film would have been an important element in bringing the film to the audience's attention as a comedy.

Like Fisher of *The Sun* many critics commented on the humour of the film as its primary selling point. 'This is a comedy about strippers, and it's funny because it understands that a stripper is also a kind of silent comedian ...' (*Times Literary Supplement*). *Time Out* also heralded the film as only designed to 'give you a good laugh'.

The Sunday quality press offered a number of different interpretations and Philip French of *The Observer* (31.8.97) remarked on the more serious messages the film conveyed: 'much of its political and sexual meaning resides in the absence of glamour and triumphalism'. French's review commented on the economical style drawing attention to the deeper political meanings of the film.

Matthew Sweet of *The Independent on Sunday* (31.8.97) remarked that 'Cattaneo doesn't attempt the mildewed detail of Ken Loach, nor the scattergun satire of *Brassed Off*, and that the 'broad comedy (is used) to make post-industrial deprivation a gender issue'. He liked the film and placed it in context of other British films to which it might be compared.

But the more sober readings of the film were not matched by Ann Billson of *The Telegraph* or Tom Shone of *The Sunday Times*. Both refused such readings and remarked that the lack of actual nudity that the title promised was something of a disappointment. Tom Shone offered that there was 'a lot of soul and chest-baring' and that, while it was a movie about 'bare bottoms, wisely, it doesn't try too hard to dress itself up as anything else'. He quotes Lindsay Law of Fox Searchlight in support of the feel-good aims over the political readings. Law is quoted as saying that it appeals to men and women differently: 'Men identify with the predicament. Women tend to laugh at the general state of men'.

National and local press reviews, together with listings magazine reviews, help to place the film in a context with other films on release at the same time or films of a similar style. Popular press reviews like that of *The Sun*

conclusion

tend to draw attention to the saleable elements, while 'quality' press reviews argue for the way the film fits into a wider context of cinema criticism. In *The Observer* and *The Independent* reviews there was reference to other films in the same tradition and opinion has differed as to how *Monty* fits with or deviates from such traditions.

Of critical interest, too, is the ways in which the trade press will review a film. *Empire*, and *Sight and Sound* are important monthly magazines offering a range of reviews of the latest films, information about directors, box office success and other related information. *Empire* (September 1997) reviewed the film as 'a comedy of sexual politics' and concluded that it was an example of 'yet another solid entry in the much appreciated movement of no-fuss, low budget British films designed to genuinely entertain'. *Empire* had an accompanying poster for the film and awarded it 3-stars in its 5-star point system.

Sight and Sound followed on with a review that begins 'Unemployment may be no joke, but *The Full Monty's* rich consistent humour derives from showing that losers who make their own luck do indeed have the last laugh.'

While *Empire* had been initially complementary but equivocal of the film's potential success, it had altered its response by November of the same year when box-office figures were rising all the time. In its second review it predicted rather differently that the film was 'well on the way towards *Trainspotting's* UK box office take of £12m. In fact, this prediction was well short of the eventual reality – nearly £48 million at the British box office alone – and when the film went to video in March 1998 *Empire* fully 'recommended' the film.

conclusion

This chapter has dealt with a range of issues relating to the context in which *The Full Monty* was released. These contexts have an important bearing on issues such as box-office success and on critical and pleasurable readings. The ways in which a film is constructed, produced, marketed and reviewed all have a bearing on how a film is likely to be received and read by an audience. It is clear in the examination of a film

conclusion

united with great success

that we need to be aware of both 'textual' features such as representation, genre and stars as well as 'extra-textual' features such as the production context and its bearing on bringing a film to a public.

In the case of *The Full Monty* these features were united with great success and the rare bringing together of these features bodes well for the recovering health of the British film industry and the success of our national cinema in the twenty-first century.

bibliography

general film

Altman, Rick, *Film Genre*,
BFI, 1999
  Detailed exploration of film genres

Bordwell, David, *Narration in the
Fiction Film*, Routledge, 1985
  A detailed study of narrative theory
  and structures

− − −, Staiger, Janet & Thompson,
Kristin, *The Classical Hollywood
Cinema: Film Style & Mode of
Production to 1960*, Routledge, 1985;
pbk 1995
  An authoritative study of cinema as
  institution, it covers film style and
  production

− − − & Thompson, Kristin, *Film Art*,
McGraw-Hill, 4th edn, 1993
  An introduction to film aesthetics for
  the non-specialist

Branson, Gill & Stafford, Roy, *The
Media Studies Handbook*, Routledge,
1996

Buckland, Warren, *Teach Yourself
Film Studies*, Hodder & Stoughton,
1998
  Very accessible, it gives an overview of
  key areas in film studies

Cook, Pam (ed.), *The Cinema Book*,
BFI, 1994

Corrigan, Tim, *A Short Guide To
Writing About Film*,
HarperCollins, 1994
  What it says: a practical guide for
  students

Dyer, Richard, *Stars*, BFI, 1979;
pbk Indiana University Press, 1998
  A good introduction to the star
  system

Easthope, Antony, *Classical Film
Theory*, Longman, 1993
  A clear overview of recent writing
  about film theory

Hayward, Susan, *Key Concepts in
Cinema Studies*,
Routledge, 1996

Hill, John & Gibson, Pamela Church
(eds), *The Oxford Guide to Film Studies*,
Oxford University Press, 1998
  Wide-ranging standard guide

Lapsley, Robert & Westlake, Michael,
Film Theory: An Introduction,
Manchester University Press, 1994

Maltby, Richard & Craven, Ian,
Hollywood Cinema,
Blackwell, 1995
  A comprehensive work on the
  Hollywood industry and its
  products

Mulvey, Laura, 'Visual Pleasure and
Narrative Cinema' (1974), in *Visual
and Other Pleasures*,
Indiana University Press, Bloomington,
1989
  The classic analysis of 'the look' and
  'the male gaze' in Hollywood cinema.
  Also available in numerous other
  edited collections

Nelmes, Jill (ed.),
Introduction to Film Studies,
Routledge, 1996
  Deals with several national cinemas
  and key concepts in film study

Nowell-Smith, Geoffrey (ed.),
The Oxford History of World Cinema,
Oxford University Press, 1996
  Hugely detailed and wide-ranging
  with many features on 'stars'

y THE FULL MONTY

Thomson, David, *A Biographical Dictionary of the Cinema,*
Secker & Warburg, 1975
  Unashamedly driven by personal taste, but often stimulating

Truffaut, François, *Hitchcock,*
Simon & Schuster, 1966,
rev. edn. Touchstone, 1985
  Landmark extended interview

Turner, Graeme, *Film as Social Practice,* 2nd edn, Routledge, 1993
  Chapter four, 'Film Narrative', discusses structuralist theories of narrative

Wollen, Peter, *Signs and Meaning in the Cinema,*
Viking 1972
  An important study in semiology

Readers should also explore the many relevant websites and journals.
Film Education and *Sight and Sound* are standard reading.

Valuable websites include:

The Internet Movie Database at
http://uk.imdb.com

Screensite at
http://www.tcf.ua.edu/screensite/contents.html

The Media and Communications Site at the University of Aberystwyth at
http://www.aber.ac.uk/~dgc/welcome.html

There are obviously many other university and studio websites which are worth exploring in relation to film studies.

the full monty

The Full Monty was released in 1997. Although it has attracted some critical attention at conferences among film scholars interested in British Cinema there is, at the time of publication, no definitive critical text available.

Beaufoy, Simon, *The Full Monty,*
ScreenPress Books, 1997
  Simon Beaufoy's original script for the film

Bordwell, David, *Narration in the Fiction Film,* Methuen & Co, USA, 1985
  Key Text on Narrative Theory

Branston, Gill and Stafford, Roy, *The Media Student's Book,* Routledge 1996
  Study guide covering issues from representation and ideology through to the development of the cinema industry

Ellis, John, *Visible Fictions,*
Routledge, London (1982, 1992)
  Good text on narrative theory with respect to audiences

Fuller, Graham, *Loach on Loach,*
(Faber, 1999)

Gledhill, Christine, *Pleasurable Negotiations* in Frances Bonner *Imagining Women: Cultural Representations of Gender,*
Polity, Cambridge, 1992

Gledhill, Christine, *Women Reading Men,* in Pat Kirkham, Janet Thumin (eds) *Me Jane: Masculinity, Movies and Women,* St Martins Press, London, 1995
  Both of Gledhill's articles discuss issues of women spectators and the question of female spectatorship

Higson, Andrew, *Dissolving Views: Key Writings on British Cinema,*
Cassell, 1997

the full monty

Key collection of writings about British New Wave cinema

Kirkham, Pat, and Thumin, Janet, 'You Tarzan' in *You Tarzan: Masculinity, Movies and Men,*
Lawrence and Wishart, London, 1993
Key collection of writings about representations of masculinity in film

Moore, Suzanne, 'Here's Looking at You Kid' in Gamman, L, and Marshment, M, *The Female Gaze,*
Women's Press, London, 1988
Writing that addresses the significance of a female gaze

Mulvey, Laura, *Visual Pleasure and Narrative Cinema,*
Screen 16(3): 6–18, 1975
Seminal article about female spectatorship

Street, Sarah, *British National Cinema,*
Routledge, London, 1997
Elaborates the ways in which British cinema has developed economically and aesthetically

Turner, Graeme, *Film as Social Practice,*
Routledge, 1993
Explores a range of issues about cinema as entertainment and as cultural event

Van Zoonen, Liesbet, *Feminist Media Studies,* Sage, London, 1994
Addresses the changes to Media Studies theory generally, with an emphasis on the ways in which representations of women's images and female audiences have been theorised

cinematic terms

audience term that refers literally to the viewer/listener or consumer, but as theorised in Media Studies it refers to how the media is understood

auteur literally from the French for 'author', it refers to the influence of the director in the creation of a film

camera shots this term refers to the distance between camera and object.

casting choosing actors to suit the parts in the film.

cause and effect a convention for organising a narrative

cinematography refers to the 'art' of shooting the film, including choices of colour, camera use etc.

closed narrative a narrative with an ending – usually film as opposed to an 'open narrative' more usually used to describe serials or soap operas

connote/connotation in semiotic theory this refers to what meaning can be deduced from a given sign, what cultural value it holds, for example rose may connote love, passion etc.

denote/denotation in semiotic theory this is the part of the sign which refers to a real world object or referent. It is the descriptive part of the analysis, for example rose denotes red flower with green stem

dissolve a term referring to the editing of a film where one shot dissolves into another

distributor company responsible for the success of the film with duties ranging from advice to the production team, marketing and publicity.

editing the process of sequencing or ordering image and sound

fade-out process of editing that marks, through fading, the transition from one shot to another

framing essentially means the ways in which a shot is composed (should be considered in conjunction with mise-en-scène, camera shots)

Frankfurt School German theorists exiled to the United States during the Second World War and who wrote about mass culture

genre term which describes how media texts can be classified into 'types'. A key aspect of the study of genre is the study of iconography

golden age the major production studios were at their most successful in the period 1930–50

iconography term that refers to the study of familiar signs (see genre)

intertextuality the ways in which media texts add meaning through reference to other media texts (an intertwining or juxtaposition of meaning)

location where films are shot. Usually refers to external locations to give sense of reality

marketing vital part of the economic process in ensuring a film makes it from production to exhibition (see distribution)

mise-en-scène a French term, drawn from theatre and referring to the design of the set. With respect to cinema, aspects of mise-en-scène are a vital aspect of both style and assist in the descriptive elements of narrative

montage process or editing where two opposing ideas are juxtaposed to produce a new meaning

THE FULL MONTY

multiplex cinema a multi-screen cinema complex

narrative this refers to the strategies used to organise a story

national cinema cinema that explicitly represents the values and ideas of the nation in which it is made. Concept of a vibrant national cinema is often linked to questions of national interest

psychoanalysis in the context of studying film these theories are used to explore the boundaries between the real and imagined worlds which join in the process of watching (see spectatorship)

realism when media texts attempt to represent the 'look' or refer to social events in the external world. Contentious idea that has its roots firmly in British film production where work led by the British New Wave in the 1960s has been dedicated to depicting life in the 'real world'

repetition and variation refers to the ways in which audiences understand texts through the repetition of familiar ideas and structures, and the ways in which genres are altered by variation

representation refers to many processes including those of construction and to the ways in which ideas are presented for audiences. Strongly linked with questions about identity, ideology, realism, stereotypes and power

restricted/omniscient narration refers to the point of view in a story and the 'voice telling' function – mostly films have 'omniscient' i.e. invisible narrators

semiotics method of analysis that distinguishes the descriptive (denotative)

aspect of a sign from the meaning (connotative) or interpretive aspect

sound effects refers to the full range of sound in a film from dialogue, sound effect to music soundtrack

space and time within the classic Hollywood narrative system, time and space are coherently represented in order to achieve the effect of reality

spectatorship process by which through 'looking' or 'gazing' we identify ourselves in the lives of the characters on the screen. Comes from psychoanalytic concepts of looking

stars literally descriptive of famous people but the term has a more complex meaning with respect to the ways that stars carry meaning for audiences. It is used with respect to narrative and genre but also marketing

stereotypes process whereby the complex characteristics of a group of people are reduced to a quickly recognised sketch

structuralism a set of theoretical perspectives that focus on structure rather than on art. The theories are predicated on analysis of 'formal' features rather than 'content'

uses and gratifications theories of audience research that foreground the 'active' element of audience interpretation

vertical integration economic term which refers to the ways in which large companies control the operations of smaller ones with connected interests. Here it is used to describe the power of the Hollywood Studio System of 1930–50 to assert control over production, distribution and exhibition

credits

written by
Simon Beaufoy

directed by
Peter Cattaneo

produced by
Uberto Pasolini

co-produced by
Paul Bucknor
Polly Leys

associate producer
Lesley Stewart

casting by
Susie Figgis

extras casting
Carole Crane
Jocelyn Cammack

locations assistant
Sarah Tapsfield

music orchestrated and composed by
Anne Dudley

first assistant director
John de Borman B.S.C.

second assistant director
Claire Hughes

third assistant director
Ben Johnson

production designer
Max Gottleib

stills photographer
Tom Hilton

costume designer
Jill Taylor

script supervisor
Cathy Doubleday

special effects
Ian Rowley

choreographer
Suzanne Grand

cast
Gaz – Robert Carlyle
Dave – Mark Addy
Lomper – Steve Huison
Guy – Hugo Speer
Horse – Paul Barber
Gerald – Tom Wilkinson
Nathan – William Snape
Jean – Lesley Sharp
Mandy – Emily Woof
Linda – Deirdre Costello

THE FULL MONTY Y